ALSO BY GABRIEL KOLKO

Vietnam: Anatomy of a Peace

Century of War: Politics, Conflicts, and Society Since 1914

*Confronting the Third World: United States Foreign Policy,
1945–1980*

*Anatomy of a War: Vietnam, the United States, and the Modern
Historical Experience*

Main Currents in Modern American History

*The Limits of Power: The World and United States Foreign
Policy, 1945–1954* (coauthored with Joyce Kolko)

The Roots of American Foreign Policy

*The Politics of War: The World and United States Foreign Policy,
1943–1945*

Railroads and Regulation, 1877–1916 (Transportation
History Prize, Organization of American Historians)

*The Triumph of Conservatism: A Reinterpretation of American
History, 1900–1916*

*Wealth and Power in America: An Analysis of Social Class and
Income Distribution*

ANOTHER CENTURY OF WAR?

GABRIEL KOLKO

THE NEW PRESS

NEW YORK
LONDON

To Joyce

Published in the United States by The New Press, New York, 2004
Distributed by W. W. Norton & Company, Inc., New York

LIBRARY OF CONGRESS CATALOGING-IN-PUBLICATION DATA
Kolko, Gabriel.
Another century of war? / Gabriel Kolko.
p.   cm.
Includes bibliographical references and index.
ISBN 1-56584-758-X (pbk.)
1. United States—Foreign relations—2001—Forecasting.
2. United States—Foreign relations—1989.
3. September 11 Terrorist Attacks, 2001—Causes.   I. Title.
E895.K65   2002
327.73'001'12—dc21   2002025512

The New Press was established in 1990 as a not-for-profit alternative
to the large, commercial publishing houses currently dominating the book
publishing industry. The New Press operates in the public interest
rather than for private gain, and is committed to publishing,
in innovative ways, works of educational, cultural, and community value
that are often deemed insufficiently profitable.

The New Press, 38 Greene Street, New York, NY 10013
www.thenewpress.com

Composition by dix!

Printed in Canada

2   4   6   8   10   9   7   5   3   1

CONTENTS

PREFACE

In 1994 I published *Century of War,* which dealt with nations of the world that had been approximately equal in military power but also had the ambition to dominate other countries. The period after 1914 was incredibly destructive, but there was also a rough symmetry of might that created some decades of tense armed standoff, intervals of peace that led inevitably to more bloody wars. The situation over the past decade has changed radically, and no nation can match the United States' military power. But its arms have not brought peace to the world even though Communism has virtually disappeared and can no longer serve to explain the behavior of the United States and its allies.

The world has become far more complex, and much more unstable politically. The Cold War is over, but the dangers and reality of wars are ever present. There are, especially, more civil wars. Weapons of every sort are more destructive and also more widely distributed. The tragic events of September 11, 2001, seemingly brought all of these disturbing factors to a climax for the first time within the United States. There were tangible reasons why they occurred—and why we now live in an era of growing insecurity that will very probably see more traumas like them as well as responses like those they evoked. In the following pages I outline some of the causes for the events of September 11 and why America's foreign policies not only have failed to exploit Communism's demise but have become both more destabilizing and more counterproductive. I also try to answer the crucial question posed in my title: Will there be another century of war?

The United States is now the sole nation with the ambition and presumably the military power and economic resources to rearrange the political destinies of states in whatever corner of the world it chooses to intervene. But this is a recipe for failure, and for more wars. Now we know that the destructive consequences of this foreign policy will reach America's very shores in ways that were unthinkable over the past century.

The United States has won the war against the Taliban in Afghanistan militarily; if the Taliban regroup and fight a guerrilla war, then what follows is even more relevant, but that is not likely to be America's concern. Then what is? Superficially, the crisis in Afghanistan may end for a period whose duration no one can predict, although the country will once again be so destabilized politically that it is very likely to reemerge as a problem for outside powers—above all, its neighbors. But Afghanistan is not a very important country. Indeed, it is a nation in name only, patched together by the British during their imperial heyday. There will be far more significant crises elsewhere, including civil wars and wars between states for which the United States has scant responsibility and in which it will play little role, if any. Such conflicts are the inevitable consequences of weapons becoming more freely available, and here the United States, the single most important arms exporter, is contributing to much of the future disorder that the world is likely to experience. But this book deals only with the United States' past and future activities, because the principal (but surely not exclusive) danger the entire world confronts is America's capacity and readiness to intervene virtually anywhere. After Afghanistan there will be more American military adventures. Ultimately the challenge is not Osama bin Laden and Muslim fundamentalism—that is more a symptom than a cause. It will not disappear until there are great changes not just in the Middle East but throughout the world, including within the United States itself. Such transformations will take decades, if they occur at all.

Technologically sophisticated American military power, which has won all the battles in Afghanistan, has only emboldened the Bush administration to use its might elsewhere. However, military success bears scant relationship to political solutions that end wars and greatly reduce the risk of their recurring. But this dichotomy between military power and political success has existed for most of the past century. The United States has always been ready to use its superior military strength even though employing that power often creates many more problems than it solves. Frequently, as Vietnam proved, unsustainable military establishments themselves become the source of America's defeats.

The United States has avenged September 11, which is the principal reason it went into Afghanistan, but the vast region from South Asia to the Persian Gulf has been shaken profoundly in the process. The region will doubtless confront these aftershocks. America may well intervene elsewhere in its futile, never-ending quest to use its military power to resolve political and social instabilities that challenge its interests as it defines them. The questions we must confront are the premises as well as the consequences of American foreign policy since the early 1950s. Such larger issues are not dependent on immediate changes that are likely to occur between the time this is written and the publication date—for example, in Indian-Pakistani relations or the permanent crisis between Israel and Palestine.

André Schiffrin of The New Press suggested this book to me shortly after September 11's tragic events, and while I absolve him of all responsibility for the views expressed here—they are wholly my own—I do want to thank him profusely for proposing it. I have reflected on, researched, and written about these issues since the late 1950s—almost a decade after I first met André—when I was a graduate student at Harvard and debated many of these questions with the men who went on to get the United States more and more deeply into war in Vietnam, a war it lost after years of anguish and destruction. These same men subsequently helped manage American foreign policy. I am well aware of the myopia, hubris, and ambition of those responsible for some of the events described here. If nothing else, Harvard transformed me into a critic of the United States' world role.

This book is dedicated to Joyce, my indispensable friend, whose companionship, stimulation, and encouragement has made everything possible.

INTRODUCTION

On September 19, 2002, President George W. Bush proclaimed the United States' commitment to fighting "preemptive" wars, unilaterally if necessary, against "rogue states" that have weapons of mass destruction or harbor "terrorists." In fact, this "new" era in international relations, with momentous implications for war and world peace, began long before then.

The disintegration of the Soviet bloc after 1990 permitted American preemptive wars and unilateralism on a scale the modern world has never seen. Earlier preemptive interventions were usually covert and incremental, and innumerable efforts at "regime changes" began no later than 1948, when the CIA helped overthrow the Syrian government. However, the United States' war against Iraq marked the first time it openly massed its military power and then invaded another nation, justifying it in the name of attaining "regime change."

The war with Iraq that began in March 2003 was but one installment of the Bush administration's ambition to recast the world. Bush also publicly identified Iran and North Korea as members of an "axis of evil," and—as the administration's "Nuclear Posture Review" to Congress made clear in January

2002—Syria and Libya are also "immediate" dangers, while China and even Russia "remain a concern."

This short book is an analysis of how and why the world has reached the most dangerous point in recent history, one full of threats of wars and instability unlike anything that existed when a Soviet-led bloc existed. The war against Iraq and those very likely to follow it are the logic of the United States' foreign and military policies that emerged in the decade following the collapse of Communism. The Bush administration has brought these policies to their logical culmination.

We now live in a world where American unilateralism has greatly increased and force has become the favored means of coping with any problems—problems that require political solutions. Washington wishes to have allies although it will not accept consultation and compromises with them; however, this is a change of degree and style rather than a basically new approach. Alliances such as NATO have been gravely and probably fatally split, a process that began well before Bush became president but which the Iraq war aggravated. The United Nations, which the White House was ready to dismiss even before America was thwarted in the bitter debate over Iraq in the Security Council, is now far less important to it than ever. Nations that were once its friends, such as France, Germany, and Russia, are now among its strongest critics.

The United States has become, as never before, a destabilizing rogue superpower led by men who instill growing fear and anxiety among friends as well as foes. Its first goal is to restructure the Muslim world, especially in the Middle East. It is presumed that elections in these nations will produce the desired outcomes, but as they revealed in Turkey, Pakistan, and Kuwait, free elections also allow the public to vent its anger at American policies, of which its virtually unwavering support for Israel is foremost. As many polls show, public opinion toward the United States has steadily become more critical virtually everywhere, not just in the Arab and Muslim nations but in Europe and Asia as well. The U.S. has never been so unpopular. From South Korea and Pakistan to Germany and France, anti-Americanism has dramatically changed the politics of nations. The war against Iraq only intensified it.

The war the United States fought in Afghanistan has left U.S.-friendly warlords in power; a nominal government exists only in Kabul. This outcome convinced many nations that had supported the Afghan war that the U.S. does not leave stability in the wake of its interventions. Afghanistan is once more the world's leading producer of opium, and home to increasingly important remnants of the Taliban and Al-Qaeda, and the war left its numerous political and economic problems still unresolved. Washington's Iraq policies caused it to smash the large coalition against terrorism built in the fall of 2001. Even more worrisome, postwar Iraq has proved to be far more costly in money and manpower than expected, and the U.S. will occupy Iraq for many years to come. Bin Laden detested Saddam Hussein's regime and there was no relationship between them, but America's war against Iraq only increased global terrorism's appeal. The world is simply far too big and complex for the United States to regulate, its formidable military power notwithstanding.

America has become militantly unilateralist, and its posture extends to innumerable issues, ranging from the blocking of a UN accord on mercury pollution in February 2003 to its higher steel tariffs and farm subsidies that imperil the future of the World Trade Organization—an organization it created.

The basic changes in its premises and the way the United States now functions in the international system have disturbed many important Americans as well as ordinary citizens. The nationalist, pseudo-religious, and neoconservative hodgepodge that serves as the intellectual justification for the Bush administration's expansive military and foreign policies has alienated more and more Americans. The polls increasingly show it, and elections may also. The CIA does not wish to produce falsehoods, which it was repeatedly asked to do regarding the non-existent connection of the Iraqi regime to bin Laden or Iraq's possession of weapons of mass destruction, both of which have or will be proven total myths. The breakup of NATO or the worsening relations with Russia and China strikes many traditional Republicans—of whom Bush's father is the most important—as folly. Even the Pentagon is full of officers critical of the expensive imperial ambitions that now hold sway in the White House. The policy of relying on military power and running up unprecedented budget deficits is not working. Even Rumsfeld conceded in a confidential October 16, 2003, memo, which was leaked immediately, that "we lack metrics to know if we are winning or losing the global war on terror." A profound crisis in confidence exists within the ranks of decision makers—exactly as there was during the Vietnam War.

How and why we have reached this dangerous impasse in human affairs, and why the world is now in sustained crisis that will endure for many years, is the subject of *Another Century of War?*

ANOTHER CENTURY OF WAR?

1

The War Comes Home

Communism virtually ceased to exist over a decade ago, depriving the United States of the primary justification for its foreign and military policies since 1945, yet America has become more rather than less ambitious. It is also far more vulnerable and insecure. September 11 confirmed that the U.S. homeland was no longer immune to the consequences of American foreign policies, and that determined enemies could attack and inflict horrendous damage upon the ultimate symbols of American power: the Pentagon and Wall Street. The perpetrators used quite simple means, but they were ready to die to accomplish their terrible ends.

Something has gone wrong, very wrong.

In an age when weapons of mass destruction have become increasingly varied and accessible, the United States is becoming more and more hated and must now pay a far greater price at home for its efforts since 1945 to intervene in the internal affairs of countless nations. The question is not only whether the risks are worth it, but also whether its attempts to control the ways countries operate have been successful in the past. Even more important, will the future be any different?

The Unlimited War to End Terror

President George W. Bush immediately declared a "war on terrorism" and threatened that "more than sixty" countries would be called to account. "The war on terror begins with al-Qaeda, but it does not end there. It will not end until every terrorist group of global reach has been found, stopped and defeated." There would be not one battle "but a lengthy campaign," and "[f]rom this day forward, any nation that continues to harbor or support terrorism will be regarded by the United States as a hostile regime." The war against terrorism, Vice President Dick Cheney predicted last October, "may never end. At least, not in our lifetime." The al-Qaeda network was global, and it would continue even if bin Laden were captured or killed. Pressed, the White House admitted that al-Qaeda's links with the many other global terrorist organizations were "amorphous."[1] So which groups and which nations were involved, and what constituted linkages? What would or could the United States do to so many nations? Did he mean Ireland, Colombia, the Philippines, Russia? Neither the president, his spokesman, nor the Pentagon was explicit. They too were amorphous as to the identity of the potential enemies.

The effort might last years and is open-ended, and its scope and goals defy predictions, even though attaining a purely military victory in Afghanistan over the Taliban regime and al-Qaeda did not pose many time-consuming challenges. After all, they were a scruffy band of essentially irregular forces based on clans and warlords of dubious loyalty, without the logistical capabilities for fighting the world's preeminent military power for very long. "[I]t may take more than two years" to attain these still-amorphous goals of uprooting terrorist networks in an indefinite number of countries, the president stated in mid-October, even though the campaign in Afghanistan might well be shorter.

By the time fifty thousand American military personnel and over four hundred aircraft were deployed from the Red Sea to the Indian Ocean, about mid-November, the Taliban's organized military formations began to capsize. The existence of Northern Alliance ground forces facing them compelled the Taliban to violate the first rule of successful warfare and to concentrate their forces, thereby giving devastating American air power vulnerable targets. Hardly any American ground forces were necessary. "[T]here are no beaches to storm, there are no islands to conquer, there are no battle lines to be drawn" in the future, the president said; yet, the military was more essential, and the risks much more subtle but greater, than ever. Even after bin Laden is killed and the Taliban defeated, Defense Secretary Donald H. Rumsfeld warned in mid-November, al-Qaeda would "be carrying on and managing those networks in a way that would be deadly to lots of people in the world." Americans now live in a "new country," President Bush warned in mid-October, and terrorism could strike them directly. Obviously, the war had reached America's shores as never before in its history—and the president assured its people that the war would continue. He gave no time limit: "[T]his is a difficult struggle, of uncertain duration."[2]

What kind of war, how great a danger, and is it worth it? Why, indeed, after the collapse of communism, is the United States in greater mortal danger than ever? About 3,000 people died in New York on September 11, and the damage was well over $35 billion; another 184 died in the Pentagon; 266 more perished on the four hijacked planes. It was, by far, the greatest loss of lives within the United States itself since the Civil War.

Some of the president's senior officials, such as Defense Secretary Rumsfeld and especially his deputy, Paul Wolfowitz, want to take the war to Iraq and remove Saddam Hussein from power. That much is definite. But what the Bush administration implied was a plan or design on their part was, in reality, very much improvisation, reflecting the administration's profound instability and confusion, a search for concrete responses to the attacks of September 11 as well as the larger question of terrorists and their alleged networks.

The military reaction to bin Laden and the Taliban was obvious. American air power was overwhelming. Initially, the United States thought it needed Pakistan's cooperation. So the Americans encouraged defections from the Taliban in the hopes of preventing the sort of power vacuum that followed the withdrawal of the Soviets in 1989. But this cumbersome effort took too much time and was largely abandoned. The selective use of air power, including B-52 carpet bombing; military pressure from the Northern Alliance; and even cash and promises to the opportunistic Pashtun chieftains and warlords within the Taliban coalition were all tried. But these tactics had to be synchronized and to mesh with one another. However, the Taliban violated the basic principles of guerrilla warfare that had brought the mujahideen success against the Soviets. During the first weeks of the war they attempted to hold most of the cities, including in non-Pashtun regions, and offered fixed targets to aircraft, which decimated them. And rather than send in large numbers of its own ground forces, the United States reluctantly decided to help the fractious Northern Alliance conquer as much territory as it could, which meant they and other anti-Taliban forces quickly took the cities. But the Alliance's principal sponsors after the mid-1990s were Iran and Russia, and the forces that constitute it have often fought one another.

Whether or not the war for the countryside will end in the same quick and easy way is debatable. On the one hand, the Taliban dissipated a great deal of material, manpower, and morale in the crucial first weeks of the war. Nor did they have help from the CIA or the Saudis, as did the mujahideen during the 1980s. But they have access to caves and mountainous terrain; they still hold a considerable amount of Pashtun territory, a region that the non-Pashtun warlords are loath to enter; and they can fight guerrilla warfare there much more effectively. By the end of November the president was warning that success "may come more slowly," "there is still a lot to be done," and American soldiers might very well get hurt in the process.[3] At the beginning of 2002 pockets of resistance remained. The war might last a long time, or it might be quite short. Only time will tell.

The ultimate political aim of creating a stable nation no longer under the domination of Islamic fanatics is infinitely more difficult than prevailing on battlefields. The sheer equation of military power assured that the United States won battles fought essentially on its terms. But the very destructiveness of this power and the speed with which it succeeded, at least in the cities, have created the very political outcome that the United States, Britain, and Pakistan initially sought to avoid: Afghanistan will remain a very troubled country that is likely to descend into more war in the coming years, just as it did after the Soviets left in 1989. For the time being, irony of all ironies, Russia has gained the most politically from the war's outcome—though this too may well change. A durable peace has not been established among the ethnic groups that constitute what is a nation in name only, and everyone who knows the area believes the situation that existed after the Soviets were defeated will reemerge in five or ten years.

The Bush administration also embarked on forging new coalitions which were—as I will detail in chapter 5—improvised and essentially ad hoc. Washington must radically change its policy toward Israel and Palestine if it is to keep the Muslim states behind its effort in Afghanistan. It will lose their cooperation and that of the Germans, French, and others if it mounts a major offensive against Iraq—much less other states—as important people in government are urging. Al-Qaeda "is just one of the networks" in innumerable countries, as the defense secretary argued, and while the war in Afghanistan was "important to the credibility" of America's efforts, it by no means ended the Pentagon's new ambitions to root out terrorism. Whether bin Laden is killed or not, terrorism will continue. Al-Qaeda may emerge largely intact from this crisis; not only has the terrorists' credibility been enhanced, but they trained about twenty thousand men in Afghanistan alone over the past decade, and they are now in many countries. There are also many Islamic jihad groups that have no connection with al-Qaeda, and they too can be found everywhere. Meanwhile, when Rumsfeld was asked how the American people were "to prepare for the next threat without knowing what the next threat is," he replied, "I wish I had a good, simple, easy answer that fit on a bumper sticker." There were many new, unfathomable dangers—in the air or water, for example—that required "a sense of heightened awareness," apprehension, and fear. "The other thing we can do is to support a government that's decided that's not the way we want to live," that will go after terrorists.[4] It is a vision that has potentially unlimited consequences and is certain to shatter old and new alliances.

A number of things were clear, however. George W. Bush assumed the presidency under a cloud, his victory coming in a much-disputed vote in Florida. His rhetoric and responses were excruciatingly vague but immensely popular. The president's approval ratings went from 55 percent just before September 11 to about 90 percent in the months after the attack. He even had the public's support to send Americans "into a long war with large numbers of U.S. troops killed or injured" and into military action against Iraq and other countries that assist or aid terrorists.[5] But he had no intention of taking this risk, and his strategy depended on air power and very minimal exposure of American boys to danger and possible death. The Democrats supported President Bush; in fact some, especially candidates for the presidential nomination in 2004, were even more hawkish. Congressional Democrats tried to compel the administration to spend a great deal more for homeland defense and rebuilding New York City. Bush had campaigned in 2000 as a critic of "big government," but after September 11 he became an "imperial" president with new, draconian powers over civil liberties. He consulted Congress much less, and his administration cut back sharply on the war news that the press could have.

Also clear was that America's foreign and military strategy and plans defined after 1990 were now topsy-turvy. "The things that were at the top of our list we're no longer paying much attention to," said Brent Scowcroft, who advised Bush's father when he was president and is still very important in official policy circles.[6] The Bush administration made foreign policy proposals that were breathtaking and open-ended, painfully and obviously vague projects and commitments whose ultimate consequences in most cases can scarcely be predicted. There were new promises but also new dangers—and we possess fifty years of experience throughout the world with which to assess them, years of successes but of even greater failures. It was these failures that led desperate men to crash planes into the symbols of American power on September 11.

What has gone wrong, and can or will the damage be undone?

Terrorism and the Indefinite Future

Terrorism has no rules; it is frequently the weapon of the weak against the strong, of the poor against the highly organized, and its victims are overwhelmingly ordinary and quite innocent people. There is success or failure, winners or losers, and if the stakes are high and one side has few weapons, then it employs what its enemies describe as terrorist methods. Many use them, and a few terrorist leaders are successful and achieve power, even becoming respectable politicians. Some, indeed, eventually denounce those who get in their way as terrorists. If we go down the list of organizations once accused of terrorism—the Irgun and Stern Gang in Palestine, the African National Congress in South Africa, and innumerable others—we will also compile a who's who of successful political movements over the past century. Terrorism will always exist because the political causes which give rise to it are integral to the way in which our world is organized.

There are, however, other forms of terrorism: police departments and the military have for decades used torture and arbitrary arrests in Argentina, Chile, Iran, Indonesia, and countless other states where human rights violations occur constantly and routinely. This is terrorism also, state sponsored, and it is much more extensive and expensive than the desperate and essentially random acts of violence that al-Qaeda and comparable groups engage in. The United States has funded, trained, and supplied dozens of state-terrorist organizations to maintain regimes that were described as anticommunist. But the United States has also supported those—like the contras in Nicaragua—that used every form of violence, including terrorism which injured and killed many innocent civilians, to overthrow established governments. I will not deal with this much more common and deadly form of terrorism here. Suffice it to say that the United States' sponsorship of this form of state terrorism is one of the crucial reasons it now has to confront violence on its own soil.

History has come full circle. Communism is dead, and today its successors in Russia and elsewhere are helping the United States extirpate the dreaded terrorists. Yesterday's freedom fighters in Afghanistan, many of them Islamic fundamentalists from other countries, are today's terrorists. There is a very good chance that in coming years we will see enemies and friends reshuffled yet again. Nothing is certain anymore; our world has become inordinately complex—not just for the onlookers but, above all, for those who seek to rule it. They cannot do so without creating more serious problems, but most believe they can—and therein lies the danger.

The monumental events of September 11, 2001, were a profound shock, both symbolically and physically, to the United States. If in the abstract a terror attack, somewhere and at some time, was fully expected, in reality no one was prepared for the magnitude or the location of these. Nothing in recent memory, perhaps nothing since the Civil War, so seared the American people's consciousness; war's front line had arrived in the United States.

The bombing of a World Trade Center underground garage in February 1993, in which six people died and hundreds were injured, had made terrorism against Americans on their own soil, not just on foreign bases, a very real possibility. Throughout the 1990s the federal government conducted several hundred planning exercises. Most of them involved chemical and biological attacks—"weapons of mass destruction" (WMD)—even though some terrorism experts insisted that low-tech hijackings or bombs against symbolic targets were much more likely. Innumerable reports, documents, and policy directives on terrorism dating back at least two decades reveal that Washington was acutely conscious of terrorism's dangers to the United States itself—at least on paper. Bombings of American bases and embassies in Saudi Arabia in June 1996, in which 19 U.S. personnel were killed and 240 were wounded, and in Kenya and Tanzania in August 1998, in which over 200 people died, reinforced what was a widely shared belief in official circles that terrorism was a clear and present danger. An American destroyer was attacked in Yemen in October 2000, killing 17 sailors. In 2001 the federal government spent nearly $800 million to predict and prepare for terrorism. Efforts ranged from abstractly calculating possible terrorist attacks to stockpiling essential equipment. Indirectly, it spent fifteen times that sum on combating terrorism, which the Pentagon also clinically dubs as "asymmetrical methods." The combined intelligence agencies' annual budget in 2001 was $30 billion, but they had no inkling of an impending attack on Wall Street or the Pentagon. Surprise, the ultimate ingredient in successful terrorism as well as warfare, was total.

The difficulty, as the U.S. Army admitted in May 1999, was that "[t]hese threats are much less predictable" than when communism existed, but the focus in official circles was overwhelmingly on chemical and biological weapons, or even nuclear bombs in suitcases—the weapons of mass destruction. When in December 2000 the CIA sought to predict global trends for the next fifteen years, it too emphasized WMD, but it also predicted they would be used "against the United States itself," and not only against its bases and companies operating abroad. The dilemma for the United States was that its precise enemy was no longer obvious, leaving it in a state of doubt that vastly complicated its calculations and its capacity both for deterring an attack and for retaliating once it has occurred. Indeed, terrorism left its justification for an antiballistic missile system, whose future cost in July 2000 was estimated as at least $60 billion over five years, in shambles. "[T]he act of terrorism taking place in the United States," then secretary of defense William S. Cohen admitted in July 2000, "is more likely than [an] intercontinental ballistic missile."[7] Such official warnings were common. There were many predictions that terrorism against the U.S. homeland itself was only a matter of when, how, and where it would occur. But few—perhaps no one in power—quite believed them.

In the weeks after the September 11 trauma the Bush administration declared a war against terrorism, without nuance and wherever it might be, and warned that more attacks were highly likely, if not certain. What the president called "a second wave of terrorist attacks" began in late September. While these attacks caused relatively few cases of anthrax in Washington, New York, and other places, they paralyzed a significant part of the federal government for at least two months and cost immeasurable amounts of time and money, giving force to the president's warnings.[8] This time the perpetrator was probably a native American who had access to the Pentagon's own high-grade biological weapons. He was independent of those who crashed the planes on September 11 and was indistinguishable from the vast mass of ordinary citizens—and therefore all the more frightening. The anthrax attack generated an immense amount of fear and affected many more people, who now feel profoundly insecure, for cranks exist everywhere, and no one can be certain whether they are benign or dangerous. And people should be worried: the technology involved is quite simple, and effective handbooks on how to make biological weapons—on a small scale, of course—have been on sale in the United States for several years. As one of them claims, "[I]f you can make Jell-O, you can wipe out cities."[9]

The press has given extensive coverage to the nation's vulnerability to various forms of nuclear attack, ranging from spent nuclear power fuel being mixed with dynamite and exploded in urban areas to nuclear power plants being destroyed and their materials released. Indeed, no form of terrorist destruction on American soil—nerve gas and germ warfare included—has been left to the imagination, and the very magnitude and horror of the September 11 attacks make them all quite credible. Moreover, the United States is not well prepared for most of them. Successive administrations have predicted terrorist attacks both within the United States and elsewhere, but the entire vast intelligence apparatus was caught by utter surprise on September 11 when a plane crashed into the Pentagon's inner sanctum and killed nearly two hundred people despite the fact that the military had twelve minutes' notice that a hijacked airliner was heading toward Washington. The innumerable warnings before September 11 were just so much hyperbole. It is very much an open question whether they will do any better the next time terrorists set out to do the American government mortal harm. We shall see, because some form of terror is very likely to happen again.

The war the United States has been fighting abroad since 1947 has reached its shores.

Who Is a Terrorist?

Terrorism is very old and very widespread, and it is an extremely complex phenomenon. The Irish Republican Army and its successors have been fighting the British for decades; they still blow up bombs in England, and Britain is America's closest ally in the war now taking place in Afghanistan. But there is also the Basque ETA in Spain, and independence movements in Kashmir, Corsica, Turkey, Sri Lanka, and elsewhere. Whether they are "terrorists" or "freedom fighters" depends wholly on one's viewpoint, because those seeking to attain political goals fight with what they have: hijacked airplanes and concealed bombs or B-52s and laser-guided rockets. But B-52s are far more destructive. For the innocent victims it is all the same, and it makes no difference how they are maimed or killed.

Much of Africa had to engage in armed struggle, including actions that were "terrorist" by their enemies' criteria, to gain independence from France, Britain, or white minorities. Some movements have the support of states, but where this is the case it is usually a marriage of convenience; most exist quite independent of them, and their raison d'être often has support from other nations. The Zionists in British Palestine are an especially notable (but not unique) example, as both American Jews and the U.S. government were crucial in this instance. Who is a "terrorist" and who is a "freedom fighter"? Above all, terrorism has causes, politics being by far the most important. While the movements deemed terrorist by their enemies often differ greatly, on the whole their adherents are far readier to die than their adversaries. The White House declared war on all terrorism after September 11, but it has admitted that the links between these groups were often "amorphous," giving itself both a universal mandate but also an escape route should some opportune alliance come to hand. Pakistan and Iran are two of the most obvious; both sustain movements others describe as terrorist. Needless to say, nations that violate human rights unconscionably, such as Uzbekistan and Pakistan, are quite acceptable if Washington considers them sufficiently useful.

The problem of who is a "terrorist" and who is a "freedom fighter" exemplifies the core of the United States' dual standard and is the heart of its present grave dilemma in the Middle East, but it has often arisen elsewhere as well. The State Department reported 138 "significant terrorist incidents" in twenty-nine nations in 2000, but this generous figure excludes Macedonia,

Northern Ireland, Israel, and a host of other places where those in authority routinely denounce as "terrorists" those who challenge them. But both of America's prime enemies in the Islamic world today—Osama bin Ladin and Saddam Hussein in Iraq—were for much of the 1980s its close allies and friends, whom it sustained and encouraged with arms and much else. Fear of the Soviet Union and, especially, of Iranian influence after the Ayatollah Khomeini took power in 1979, has repeatedly caused successive administrations in Washington to encourage and support extremists—whether Sunni fundamentalists or secular but consummately ambitious tyrants like Saddam Hussein. The consequences have been chaos—political, military, and ideological—and America is now paying for it.

The United States began to aid "freedom fighters" in Afghanistan after the Soviets invaded it in December 1979, always in close alliance with the rulers of Saudi Arabia, who had both money and a puritanical theology, Wahhabism, to provide motivation. The CIA spent $3 billion in Afghanistan throughout the 1980s, more than all of its other covert programs combined. The Saudis contributed almost as much and, even more important, provided as many as fifteen thousand young Saudis to fight against the Soviet invaders and their local allies, who are today the backbone of America's friends in the Northern Alliance. One of these Saudis, very well connected to the Saudi elite and a person of great talent as well as a fanatical Muslim, was Osama bin Laden, who was in charge of funneling money, men, and arms into Afghanistan. While the U.S. and Pakistani intelligence and military administered most of this effort, and Pakistan made certain that much of this aid was funneled to friendly Pashtuns in anticipation that they would become the dominant influence in that beleaguered nation once the Russians were driven out, there is no question that bin Laden had Saudi authorization for his heavy responsibilities. Without this massive amount of American funding and weapons there was no possibility of defeating the Soviets militarily. Muhammad Omar, who eventually became the leader of the Taliban, was a subcommander and "freedom fighter" during this period.

It was in this context, where no questions were asked, that bin Laden built his al-Qaeda terrorist network, based heavily on foreign Muslims who had been trained in Afghanistan, and learned how to operate effectively in many dozens of nations—Albania, Bosnia, Kashmir, and Chechnya were the best known but by no means the only ones. But apart from existing in many places and having links with terrorist networks with similar objectives, personalities are not decisive; if anyone succeeds in killing bin Laden, there are many who could replace him, perhaps even more ably. There is so much money connected with criminal networks—drugs above all—that people linked with him have every incentive to keep his network alive. For almost a decade all of the Western intelligence services have known of this unique mixture of Muslim fundamentalism, drugs and criminality, and readiness to fight in separatist causes. The Kosovo Liberation Army (KLA) was the best known of these, and although the United States initially denounced it in 1998 as a "terrorist group," the following year it allied itself with the KLA, its well-known drug and criminal activities and its irredentist ambitions in Macedonia notwithstanding, just as in Afghanistan and Bosnia the United States first employed those who later filled al-Qaeda's ranks.[10] It took September 11 to prove to the United States that the Islamic fanatics had their own agenda and that it had been colossal folly for it to make such alliances. That event and its aftermath made bin Laden all the more influential, even if he is killed, because no one has filled the role of a hero among the Arab masses since the eclipse of the Arab nationalist movement well over a decade ago.

Afghanistan was scarcely the only place that the CIA produced "blowback," its expression to describe its foreign proxies who then turn on the United States and its interests—the unintended consequences of covert operations. President Ronald Reagan's "war on terrorism" meant arms for the contras in Nicaragua, who also peddled drugs to raise funds. On the other hand, Manuel Noriega, CIA asset who was commander of the Panamanian Defense Forces and became that tiny but strategic nation's ruler, eventually required a brief American invasion in late 1989 to end his huge drug operations. But the most important scene of U.S. operations was in the Middle East, and especially the Persian Gulf, where the stake is control over the larger part of the world's oil reserves. Bin Laden made this concern all the more certain by his turning on the absolutist, authoritarian Saudi elite that had sponsored him. The half million infidels who entered the kingdom to defeat the Iraqi invasion of Kuwait, which began in August 1990, and the approximately five thousand American troops who remain until this day (plus a larger group of civilians who are connected with the military), as well as the air attacks on Iraq since its defeat, made him an enemy of the existing regime in the name of Islam. In 1994 the Saudis stripped him of his citizenship, although he still retains very important friends and sympathizers within the elite. Saudi Arabia was one of only three nations to recognize the Taliban regime in Afghanistan, and there exists a close affinity between the two forms of Islam—which has made the regime an extremely unreliable ally for the United States. Were people who agree with bin Laden to succeed there, it would open a Pandora's box of potential problems for Washington in a region absolutely vital to America's economic and strategic interests.

The mood of crisis that has engulfed the United States since the tragic September 11 attacks on the World Trade Center and the Pentagon has its roots in a history that goes back nearly a half century. Given its causes, such a crisis was virtually inevitable. The United States has advised as well as fought many wars everywhere in the world since 1947—two major conflicts, in Korea and Vietnam, but dozens of others, covert as well as public.

But the United States itself is now on war's front line—and it will remain there permanently.

2

THE MIDDLE EAST:
THE LEGACIES OF FAILURE

Oil has not been the sole factor guiding U.S. foreign policy in the Middle East, but free access to the region's enormous reserves—now about two-thirds of the world's known supply—has been its most consistent and overriding concern. Other considerations have at various times been important, of course, but they have simply not been of the same significance. The events of September 11 were the direct result of over fifty years of American involvement in the region, the consequence of actions and policies that have destabilized the arc of nations extending from the Mediterranean to South Asia. Today we live with these outcomes. The United States has its oil, but the region is profoundly troubled—and so is the entire world.

The Middle East was the region where the intrinsic ambiguities of the United States' relationship with Great Britain, its closest military and ideological ally, shaped all of its actions. Although it sought not to weaken Britain either economically or militarily—on the contrary, it loaned England huge sums after August 1945 precisely because it wanted a barrier to Soviet influence ranging from Europe to the Indian Ocean—the United States also wanted far greater control over the region's oil reserves. The two nations were the sole rivals for the single most important ingredient in a modern industrial society, but the Truman administration believed it was very much in the United States' interest that the British continue their military role in the region; if they did not police it, then Washington would have to fill the vacuum. Elements of genuine friendship as well as competition characterized U.S. actions throughout the period ending about 1956, when the two nations irrevocably parted ways in the region. But domestic political pressures (especially from ambitious oil companies and the powerful pro-Zionist lobby), the formal American ideological opposition to trading regions which excluded it, and the growing need for access to the region's oil made America's desire not to weaken the British far more rhetoric than reality.

Ideologically, at least, the British had a great deal in common with the United States. The two nations were rivals for control over the region's oil, and each favored its own clients, but British obstinacy and arrogance made it much easier for America to gradually supplant Britain's dominating role in the area. And Britain could not afford the price of being an imperial power, placing it at a decisive disadvantage in dealing with the Americans. As early as 1946, London asked the United States to take over its costly aid to the Greek regime, and it was in this context that in March 1947 the Truman Doctrine was declared and the domino theory was first articulated; aid was also extended to Turkey, and Washington warned that the Middle East, with its "great natural resources," and even Asia were at stake.[1]

Until 1948 the United States even supported the beleaguered British position in Palestine, where Zionist terrorists cost the British many lives; but the presidential election compelled Truman reluctantly to play an independent role. What the British wanted most was assurances from the State Department that it would not help American oil firms challenge the 1928 "Red Line agreement," which formalized Britain's dominant position—Saudi Arabia excluded—in the Middle East's oil industry. Events were to show that they were not to get it, either verbally or in reality. Both Iran and Iraq—setting a precedent that other states in the region followed—sought to entice American firms to counterbalance British predominance, and the bait was too tempting. Even though officially Washington favored continued collaboration with England, and certainly wanted Britain after 1948 to assume responsibility for the Middle East's military security, the cooperation it proposed was increasingly on its own terms. But it was not only access to oil that motivated American actions. The United States also feared a vacuum of power wherever the weakened British Empire was capsizing—ranging as far as South Asia—into which an amorphously defined communist influence could enter.

Oil provided the context in which the Americans placed their concern over the decline of British power, and thereby accelerated it principally for the nobly intended sake of geopolitics rather than the profit of American oil firms. The United States had been a net exporter of oil before 1939; but by 1946 it was clear that America would import an ever greater share of its petroleum needs, and by 1960 it purchased nearly one-fifth of its oil from foreign sources. Even before extensive exploration, in 1946 the Middle Eastern reserves were almost equal to the entire Western Hemisphere's, and its output went up exponentially. By 1950 its reserves were equal to the rest of the world's combined—and the British controlled most of it. Everyone knew that the Middle East held the key to the future of the world's oil industry, and Middle Eastern oil also cost far less than American to locate and extract.

The Korean War accelerated the U.S. abandonment of the British. The United States concluded that "ultranationalists" were the greatest danger and that the British were strengthening their influence by refusing to pay higher royalties—the 50-50 split that U.S. firms had initiated with Venezuela in 1948. The minor Communist threat in these nations could be handled with stronger "police controls." What was essential was a British willingness to pay the Arab states greater shares for their oil. Secretary of State Dean Acheson later recalled that "in an unplanned, undesired, and haphazard way" the United States supplanted the British in the area. But there was nothing unplanned in the CIA's helping General Naguib el-Hilali overthrow King Farouk—a docile British puppet—in July 1952, which brought Colonel Gamal Abdel Nasser to power. The U.S. agents dealing directly with Nasser sympathized with his commitment to a period of discipline to purge Egypt of its royalist inheritances—and stifle whatever Communists existed.[2] The single most important British bastion, through which its canal to its Asian empire flowed, was now under American influence.

In Iran, however, the United States decided to openly undercut the British, who controlled the Anglo-Iranian Oil Company (AIOC), and to prevent the nationalist Muhammad Mossadegh from coming to power. Mossadegh, who headed a crucial committee of the Majlis (parliament) and was the most visible exponent of the popular proposal for nationalizing the AOIC, was European-educated and played to the urban middle classes. While he was opportunistic (politicians everywhere suffer from this malady) and willing to utilize the Communist Tudeh Party, he was also an anticommunist who was eager to modernize Iran in a vague but fairly conventional bourgeois fashion. The Americans favored the young shah, who courted them to offset the British and Russians and who shared their utter dislike of Mossadegh's nationalism. Since Iran was virtually bankrupt, and the British paid 10–12 percent royalties while the U.S. firms agreed to a 50-50 split in neighboring Saudi Arabia in 1950, the die was cast. The American ambassador in Tehran thought the British were "self-righteous and arrogant."[3] In early 1951 they reluctantly agreed to 50-50, but it was too late; the Majlis nationalized the AIOC in March, and Mossadegh became prime minister the following month.

While the Pentagon feared the change might increase Soviet influence, the State Department at first encouraged Mossadegh's intransigence, and the British, with ample reason, thought the Americans were openly undermining their position. During 1952, however, the United States wavered because the Mossadegh government created mounting economic disorder and the Communists became stronger; in July and again in November Washington offered Iran a $100 million advance if it would permit U.S. firms to handle its oil, but the British were able to block it. Mossadegh, who also feared growing turmoil and was strongly anti-Soviet, was naively convinced that he could play Britain against America to obtain his goals. By this time the United States saw Iran mainly as a dangerous island of instability which the Soviets could exploit, while the British were worried principally about the future of the empire and their payment balances—oil.

When Eisenhower became president in January 1953 he authorized the CIA to cooperate with a British plan to overthrow Mossadegh. London successfully stressed the Communist danger, but Washington also decided that it would take over the once crucial British role. The following August, despite mishaps which almost produced failure, the shah was installed as a virtual dictator. Working under a deadline to force the British hand, the Iranians hired the former head of Texaco to advise them, while the official American representative to the renewed oil negotiations was a former consultant to major American oil companies. Five major U.S. firms got 40 percent of the new company; even the shah disliked the new terms, but the British were the major losers.

By far the most important problem that America confronted in the Middle East was not the Soviet Union but its relations with England, for not only were the Communist parties inconsequential but the region's social and political dynamics were far more complex than elsewhere. The British were removed step-by-step, but the labyrinthine cultural and political factors which were playing themselves out far transcended America's capacity to comprehend, much less control.

In Iran, which was of crucial importance both strategically and economically, the United States opposed and overthrew a nationalist, largely middle-class movement which was neither authoritarian nor traditionalist. These nationalists might have done so inefficiently, but they were more likely than any of the alternatives to modernize the nation. In Iran the United States placed all of its bets on the shah and thereby made a grievous error. Elsewhere in the Persian Gulf the United States supported feudal and authoritarian regimes, all strongly traditionalist. American policy was not merely convoluted but entirely opportunistic. The British leaders who later wrote memoirs bitterly portrayed the Americans as anti-British; in fact, they were more likely simply pro-American. What was crucial in the long run was that secular movements of political, social, and ideological change either were repressed—and here the American role was crucial in buttressing traditionalist regimes—or discredited themselves. Thus, rebellion and discontent throughout the Middle East increasingly took fundamentalist Islamic forms and its ideologies. Some of these were syncretic and quite irrational, but they had a broader mass appeal than modernist and middle-class ideologies, and most were deadly serious in their fanaticism. Terrorism was one of the outcomes.

The United States replaced Britain only insofar as control over oil was concerned. Otherwise there was almost no improvement in the fate of the people or the kinds of political orders that controlled them. The large majority of people in the Middle East needed and often desired elementary social services and rights, but anyone who spoke for their cause was likely to be treated as a subversive. Only the mosque was an acceptable locale for dissent. Instead of developing gradually politically or ideologically, the region remained locked in ignorance and authoritarianism, and repression became the rule—with American endorsement of most of it. There were some exceptions, of course, but they were not sufficient to avert the crisis that is racking the United States and the Middle East today.

The United States Traumatizes the Region

The United States was convinced it had to confront the nationalism which spread throughout much of the Middle East after the late 1940s, and this it did unevenly and often uncomfortably. By 1962 five countries were ruled by the military, who comprised the large majority of the new leaders. That they were anti-British was axiomatic, but Marxism's influence was negligible, and the politically astute men who led these movements knew how to play on cold war rivalries to optimize the military and economic aid they received from both sides. Syncretic ideologies were the rule, and while these leaders were opposed to Islamic traditionalism and monarchies they also tended to be inefficient, unstable, and corrupt.

In Egypt the United States supported Nasser, who became formal head of the nation in November 1954 and spent the next two years trying to consolidate his precarious domestic political position. Nasser played on divisions among American decision makers, but they all had no doubt he was, in his own way, staunchly anti-Soviet. The Saudis gave him financial support; Nasser merely attempted to get the West and Russians, as British foreign secretary Harold Macmillan later put it, "to bid up each other's price."[4] Nasser miscalculated and alienated the United States in May 1956 by recognizing Communist China, and two months later Washington canceled an offer to loan Egypt money to build the Aswan Dam. Then, at the end of July, Nasser seized and nationalized the Suez Canal, Britain's lifeline to the Persian Gulf and its former empire. Britain's leaders were certain that the Eisenhower administration had encouraged their plans to invade Egypt in conjunction with the French and

Israelis, but in fact the United States favored a negotiated reso-
lution of the dispute—there was a presidential election in November. The attack on Egypt began at the end of October, and
the United States immediately opposed it. The alliance with
Britain and France, it stated clearly, applied only to Europe; at
the beginning of December, bowing to the United States working through the United Nations, the British ignominiously
withdrew from Egypt. Thus their once dominant role in the
vast region ended.

The result was a vacuum and a vastly increased American
role. In January 1957 Eisenhower proclaimed his doctrine that
the United States was ready to protect any country requesting
aid "against overt armed aggression from any nation controlled
by international communism," a vague formulation that created
altogether new problems for the Americans. Lebanon, Syria,
Jordan—the region was destabilized as never before, and between 1956 and 1965 U.S. military forces greatly increased their
interventions in the region. Some of these were huge. In
Lebanon in July 1958, fourteen thousand troops equipped with
atomic artillery landed. Now U.S. credibility was at stake in a far
more unstable political environment than the region had ever
experienced—officers overthrew the pro-British Iraqi monarchy at the same time. No Middle Eastern nation, then or
thereafter, ever became Communist, and the word itself was
meaningless in the regional context. But not only American
spokesmen abused it; in March 1959 Nasser accused the officers
ruling Iraq of introducing "a Communist reign of terror." [5]

The problem, which many American officials admitted
in private, was that Arab political complexities and changes
transcended the United States' ability to master them, so the

Americans might be just as victimized by the region's social and political dynamics as the British. Still, although Congress, over Eisenhower's and Dulles's objections, gave Israel modest sums of economic aid in the form of grants and loans, largely because of the Zionist bloc's skill in mobilizing Congress's ethnic voting coalition and the Democrats, the United States had managed to avert the shoals of the Arab-Israeli conflict for well over a decade. It also banned arms deliveries to Israel and Jordan. But Israel's lesser importance at this time was due principally to the indifference of Middle Eastern states after 1949 to the Palestinian-Arab cause. This was to change. Nothing lay before the United States save far deeper troubles.

Those difficulties began in the spring of 1967 and culminated in June, when Israel embarked on its "Six-Day War" and conquered the remainder of pre-1948 Palestine as well as Syria's Golan Heights. Israel's actions were in large part a response to demagogic rivalries among the Arab states, which led to Syrian shelling of Israel from the Golan, an Egyptian blockade of the Gulf of Aqaba, and other clear provocations. Guerrilla activity during preceding years was only a nuisance to the Israelis but it gave them a convenient excuse to expand their territorial control over pre-1948 Palestine and the Golan. The war ended because of Moscow's threats and a tense, potentially very dangerous U.S.-Soviet naval standoff. But it also initiated a regional arms race which allowed the Soviets, for the first time, to play a major role in the area. In January 1968 the United States lifted its embargo and began massive arms aid to Israel. This aid reached $600 million in 1971 (seven times the amount under the entire Johnson administration) and over $2 billion in 1973. Thenceforth, Israel became the leading recipient of U.S. arms aid. Today it still receives about $3 billion in free American aid. Most of the Arab world, quite understandably, has since identified Israel and the United States as one.

The British decision in December 1967 to withdraw all its forces from the Persian Gulf region by the end of 1971 left the United States alone, with immense obligations, when it was deeply involved in the Vietnam War and scarcely in a position to fill the vacuum. American relations with Israel had been friendly but discreet until then, but Washington began to look for surrogates or proxies that could help it create barriers to the Soviet Union—which was unwilling to employ its own troops but ready to heavily arm states such as Egypt, Syria, and Iraq. The CIA before the June 1967 war told the various administrations that Israel could defeat its neighbors even if they combined to fight together. The State Department warned that Arab nationalism was a greater threat than the USSR, but successive administrations ignored its opinion.

Israel and Iran, and later Saudi Arabia, were designated the United States' closest allies in the region, where five major American firms controlled half the entire oil output at a time that both the demand for and price of oil were rising. Washington believed relying on surrogates was a solution to its regional challenges; in reality, this reliance only increased its problems. The United States now had to defend and stabilize its proxies, expanding its definition of credibility to include their security. In doing so it further inflamed Arab nationalism. From this point onward, however, Washington subordinated all regional issues to what it believed was an overriding Soviet-American rivalry. Israel increasingly held a de facto veto over American policy on the Palestinian-Arab question. When on October 6,

1973, the Egyptians overwhelmed a completely surprised Israeli army in the Sinai, America united with the Russians in the UN to end the fighting. But it still regarded the USSR as its main enemy in the region rather than as a victim of the Arab world's cynical willingness to exploit it for arms. Not a single Communist state was established in the region, and it should have been perfectly obvious that Arab nationalism—which united the virtually medieval Saudis and secular Arabs—was far more potent than leftist radicalism. Of far greater and enduring importance was a massive Saudi and Gulf oil boycott which increased oil prices by 1979 to almost twenty times the 1970 level and had immense repercussions for the world economy.

After 1967, the Arab-Israeli conflict guaranteed that anti-Americanism would only intensify. The quickening cycle of change and crisis, combined with the Middle East's crucial importance as supplier of the world's oil, meant that the region would increasingly frustrate the United States and that it, in turn, would alienate the Arab world. Given the vast responsibilities in the area it decided to assume, and its need to depend upon surrogate regimes, only crises lay before it.

America's Failure: The Iran Crisis

Iran was to confirm the fact that the United States was no stronger than its proxies. Assuming Britain's lucrative rights but complex responsibilities in Iran was one of the most crucial actions that America was to take in the Middle East. It eliminated a secular, middle-class nationalism, but it had no idea that it would also have to confront profound changes in that nation. The United States overthrew those who favored modernizing options and left a resurgent Muslim fundamentalism as the status quo's main opponent. No other nation in the Middle East better illustrated the risks to the United States when it depended on proxies to protect its interests.

The shah was anti–British, but he understood thoroughly America's geopolitical goals in the region and how he might exploit them to reinforce his power. He relied on the military to sustain his regime, and over time his police also became crucial—especially after 1962, when he assumed virtually total power. He bypassed the nationalist middle classes and intelligentsia, and during the early 1960s some American officials worried that he was politically too isolated. By introducing an inept and corruptly managed land reform intended to end virtual feudalism in many areas, he instead added to the rural society's problems and drove many peasants into the cities. By 1963 his main opposition came from the traditionalist, fundamentalist Shiite religious leaders, the mullahs, of whom the Ayatollah Ruhollah Khomeini was the most important; the shah was not a Shiite. Riots in the major cities in the summer of 1963 resulted in over a thousand deaths and increasing repression, which became the shah's way of retaining power. After 1971 the CIA and the Israeli Mossad helped train SAVAK, his dreaded security organization. Thousands filled Iranian prisons, and the press, media, and universities were tightly controlled. Washington depended on the shah, and its reliance on him increased after 1967, when the British decided to leave the Gulf.

The shah courted the Americans successfully, but he also wanted greater oil revenues and more sophisticated arms, and he even threatened to turn to the USSR if he could not buy them from the United States. He shrewdly encouraged

America's geopolitical visions and fears for the region, but he also increased his oil revenues until 1976. He even announced in early 1973 that he would not renew the 1954 oil agreement when it expired in 1979—in effect, nationalizing oil and following in Mossadegh's footsteps. But he also spent $20 billion on overpriced American arms from 1970 through 1978, providing a market for one-quarter of U.S. arms exports. Corruption and repression suffused his regime, and the shah and his family amassed a huge fortune. By 1977 some 7,200 American military personnel and contract employees helped service his modern army, but the living standards for the large majority of Iranians fell. The visible class differences helped to traumatize the people further.

There was no class basis for the shah's regime, only the army and its satraps—and their ultramodern equipment. In September 1978 the CIA predicted the shah would remain in office over the next decade, even though bloody confrontations between Muslims and the police had begun earlier that year. In the fall of 1978 the opposition to the shah took to the streets, and the army learned that it could not depend on its poorly paid conscripts from the villages. It took only several months for the army to disintegrate. The rest was certain. The shah went into exile in January 1979, and on February 5 Khomeini took power and Iran became an Islamic republic. It was a major, total defeat for American policy in the Middle East, the most important it has ever experienced in that region.

The Carter administration's intense dissatisfaction turned to fury in November, when Iran's new leaders seized fifty-two Americans working in the embassy. Never had the United States suffered such humiliation. The following January it proclaimed the "Carter Doctrine," which threatened any "outside force" seeking "to gain control of the Persian Gulf region" with an unspecified but possibly nuclear response anywhere in the world should America's "vital interests" be attacked. The Carter Doctrine was not a policy but an impotent and pathetic stance; the problem was not the Soviet Union but a very militant Islamic movement. Communism was irrelevant, and a botched American effort in April 1980 to free the hostages only added to its discomfort. Having pushed the British out and taken on the immense task of seeking to control the Middle East, the United States had no means for doing so. Like Britain before it, it now confronted the region's immense complexities.

The Reagan administration picked up the gauntlet Iran had thrown down, and its chosen instrument was the secular Saddam Hussein, who became the virtual dictator of Iraq in July 1979. Indeed, he had even begun his career with vaguely socialist pretensions, which were then in vogue among officers, but he was ultimately completely opportunistic. Power, not ideology, was his sole concern. He not only detested Islamic fundamentalism but also had ample reasons to consider Iran an enemy: in the 1960s Iran had begun to supply Kurdish dissidents with arms, and it had seized strategic Iraqi islands in 1971 (leading to a break in diplomatic relations). So the United States, beginning under Carter, encouraged Saddam to confront the Iranian bullies, who were overarmed with American weapons, by secretly giving Iraq false intelligence on alleged Iranian weaknesses. In the sordid war that followed, successive American administrations also gave Iran some assistance—indeed, the CIA helped to funnel U.S. aid to the contras in Nicaragua by secretly selling arms to Iran via Israel. But most of its effort went to aid Iraq—and Sad-

dam Hussein. Still, the United States helped Iran enough to pro-
tract the war, and proved a devious ally to both sides. Iraq was set
up to fight a war it could not win, one that ended by benefiting
only the United States, its reactionary neighbors, and arms merchants all over the world.[6]

Washington, Kuwait, and Saudi Arabia strongly encouraged
Saddam to invade Iran in late 1980 in the expectation that Iraq
would annex part of Iran and help prevent the charismatic Shi-
ites from extending their influence throughout the region and
challenging the no less conservative Sunni fundamentalist doctrine, of which the Saudis consider themselves the principal de-
fenders. As then president George Bush put it in early 1992, "As
you may remember in history, there was a lot of support for Iraq
at the time as a balance to a much more aggressive Iran under
Khomeini."[7] But Iran had much greater manpower, and the
war took far longer than expected. Iraq borrowed $95 billion,
mainly from Saudi Arabia and Kuwait, and imported $42 bil-
lion in arms. The United States supplied Iraq with intelligence
throughout the war and provided it with more than $5 billion
in food credits, technology, and industrial products, most coming after it began to use mustard, cyanide, and nerve gases
against both the Iranians and dissident Iraqi Kurds. Both sides
wrecked each other's refineries, and at the beginning of 1987,
with Iran desperate and angry at Kuwait for funding the war,
the United States put its own flag on Kuwait's tankers and provided its navy's protection for them, increasing the U.S. war-
ships in the gulf from six to at least forty by September 1987.
Indeed, had the United States not done so, the Kuwaitis and
Saudis threatened to dump their vast holdings of U.S. Treasury

bonds. A cease-fire was signed in August 1987, and a tense, disputatious peace has existed since then. At least 370,000 people died, 262,000 of them Iranians; but Iran claimed 800,000 dead. No one really knows how to measure accurately such horrors. The war cost Iran over $600 billion directly and in lost oil and export income; Iraq spent almost as much and owed its neighbors vast sums. Both nations were devastated.

The United States was Iraq's functional ally and encouraged it to build and utilize a huge army with modern armor, aviation, artillery, and chemical and biological weapons. It did not foresee what was obvious: Saddam could also use his advanced arms in other ways. But the profusion of modern arms in so many hands was far more than commerce for arms manufacturers. It also transformed power relations in the Middle East and made the world far more dangerous.

Oil: The Middle East's Stakes

What stakes are involved in the Middle East? Some data are relevant at this point.

The United States produced 69 percent of the petroleum it consumed in 1970 but 38 percent in 1996. After the early 1980s its production in absolute terms began falling, and its crude oil imports became even more crucial. From 1960 until 1996 its imports rose at least fourfold. Most of its imports after 1945 were from Western Hemisphere sources and Nigeria, but the Persian Gulf region supplied 10.1 percent of U.S. imports in 1983 and 23.8 percent in 2000—most of it from Saudi Arabia.

For Western Europe and Japan the percentages are far higher. The Persian Gulf in 2000 contained approximately 65 percent of the world's total oil reserves and about 34 percent of its natural gas reserves. The region has become increasingly important for the entire world economy.

Projections are always subject to correction, some crucial, but domestic U.S. petroleum production until 2020 is expected to remain constant. Its consumption over the period 1998–2020 is projected to rise from 18.9 to 25.8 million barrels daily, and all of this increase must be imported. But the competition for imports will become far more intense, especially from China. The Persian Gulf states will always be eager to sell their oil, but that they already control the single most crucial factor in modern industrial power—and are likely to increase their leverage in the future—is a fact of which those in power in Washington are acutely aware.[8] Both the president and the vice president have worked in the oil industry.

The Gulf War and Its Aftermath

No sooner had Iraq's war with Iran ended than Kuwait began pressing Baghdad for repayment of its huge loans. It also demanded that Iraq abandon its border dispute with Kuwait, and it lowered greatly the world price of oil, virtually Iraq's only source of hard currency, by exceeding its OPEC output quota. The Iraqi army occupied Kuwait in August 1990, and it now became its former allies' detested enemy. For a decade the United States, Kuwait, and Saudi Arabia had pursued a political strategy in the Gulf which was now a consummate failure; it had backfired disastrously. They had financed and supported

Iraq as a balance to Iran, and to destroy Saddam Hussein's forces was to produce the very outcome it had been American policy to avoid: Iran became the dominant power in the absolutely vital Gulf region, and Iraq's action produced a vacuum that assured that Iran would remain the principal long-term threat to U.S. interests.

Washington began planning for war with Iraq no later than October, intending to destroy Saddam's elite Republican Guard. Operation Desert Storm began January 17, 1991. Saddam was an astonishingly convenient and stupid enemy who followed the rules of conventional warfare, and over forty-seven days, air power largely—but not entirely—decimated his army and the modern equipment the Kuwaitis and Saudis had financed. Three hundred eighty thousand American soldiers and as many allied forces were used against 183,000 Iraqis in Kuwait alone; a total military victory came very quickly. Only the Kuwaitis favored the American-led forces driving all the way to Baghdad, which they could easily have done, but the coalition would have disintegrated. Saddam Hussein remains in power after a decade, and Iraq is a pariah state under UN sanctions, still subject to U.S. and British air attacks. Iraq's debts are now astronomical, making it the world's most indebted nation, and it is unlikely they will be fully paid. The United States remains Saddam's archenemy and believes that he is attempting to develop chemical, biological, and other weapons of mass destruction. He surely had ample help from Western nations in doing so when his target was Iran. If it is true, and it may be, then he may use them against American interests in ways that cannot be predicted.

Civilian deaths as a result of the U.S.-led war against Iraq are subject to radically different estimates, for there are no accurate census takers of the atrocities of the past century. As many as thirty-three thousand civilians died during the short war and the Kurdish and Shiite rebellions that followed. Estimates of the number of civilians who have died over the past decade as a result of UN sanctions (which the United States has supported more strongly than any nation) on absolutely vital imports of food and medicine range from one hundred thousand to a half million. These figures, shocking as they are, are still much lower than the casualties Iraq inflicted upon Iran with enthusiastic Kuwaiti, Saudi, and American support.

The brief American war with Iraq—so easy in large part because Saddam is an incompetent military strategist—ended the occupation of Kuwait but created far more important difficulties for the victors, above all Saudi Arabia. For Saudi Arabia is a very troubled and increasingly unstable nation. It is ruled as a result of a 1744 alliance between the al-Saud family, which holds political power, and the al-Wahhab family, which runs the state religion along exceedingly conservative, puritanical lines and is in charge of Islam's holiest sites. The clergy retains immense power and prestige. This hereditary arrangement is a gross anachronism in every sense. It has left the vast majority of locals, including the increasing proportion of educated males (women have no rights whatsoever and very few can work or even drive), politically impotent. There have been increasingly articulate and important attempts to challenge the monarchy's absolute power, but reforms during the 1990s in the form of consultative bodies changed nothing. The ruling family itself (which numbers about seven thousand) is divided, the succession is unclear, and some parts of it are supporters of dissidents such as Osama bin Laden. The large majority of the labor force is composed of foreign workers (seven million of the twenty-two million population), who have no rights, but the majority are Muslims. The per capita income, reflecting the drop in oil revenues, has fallen by almost two-thirds since the early 1980s, and this also has fueled discontent. But the Saudis still spend enormous sums proselytizing the Islamic world and fighting Shia and similar heresies.

There is growing dissatisfaction with the basic political structure, a good part of which has taken religious forms, and dissent has expanded greatly over the past decades. Indeed, opposition in the guise of religion is the only legally tolerated form of dissent in much of the Arab world, and Islamic purist extremism is to a crucial extent a reflection of this fact. The royal family lives ostentatiously abroad, and there are sharper class distinctions and consciousness than ever. There is now a critical clergy, but Wahhabism still remains a charismatic religion. Its contradiction, however, is that many of its most radical followers are poor young men whose motives and ideals are essentially hostile to the existing elites' hegemony, including in Saudi Arabia. In this unstable context, bin Laden has been highly successful in recruiting followers and raising money. With the encouragement of all religious tendencies, up to fifteen thousand young Saudis went to Afghanistan to fight with the mujahideen against Soviet troops during the 1980s. Bin Laden, who was very well connected with the elite, was chosen by the head of Saudi intelligence to help command them.

It was during the 1980s that the CIA worked closely with the Saudis to fund the war against the Soviets in Afghanistan, and they nearly matched the $3 billion that the Agency itself spent. Many of bin Laden's wealthy Saudi contacts, motivated by similar religious convictions, a sense of guilt, or the like, continued to fund him over the following decade. They presently include members of the extended royal family unhappy with current trends and the possible succession. In any case, the United States welcomed Islamist movements as an antidote to secular leftist groups, which they feared would work with the Soviets, just as it preferred the shah in Iran to secular middle-class nationalists.

The Gulf War brought to a head these tensions, which essentially revolve around the question of how a virtually medieval but very rich society should interact with modern realities, and tensions have only sharpened since then. Bin Laden proposed that a purely Islamic army, such as he had formed in Afghanistan, could drive the Iraqis out of Kuwait and—above all—defend Saudi Arabia, and that foreigners were not needed on holy Saudi soil. The ruling family preferred that the Americans confront Iraq, but it also increased its purchases of sophisticated military equipment, a step that divided the elite. Saudi Arabia for years has been the leading market for American arms. But this also meant accepting—for an indefinite duration—a much more visible presence of U.S. troops, along with their rules and conspicuous manners. American military personnel and support in that country peaked at about thirty thousand but are now reduced to approximately five thousand, plus a larger number of American civilians to service the ultramodern Saudi army. Bin Laden could build a following in this heady context, and he especially opposed the stationing of Americans—which led to his being stripped of his citizenship in 1994. He has concocted an inchoate chiliastic and syncretic alternative to the ruling elite and its theology, but his intense hostility to all foreign influences is one that emerges logically from the official

Wahhabi doctrine—with which his differences are more of degree than of kind—and resonates sufficiently throughout the nation to provide him with many followers and ample funds. This mixture of theology and rebellion against authority also appealed to many Muslims in other nations, and it replaced various socialist notions as the dominant expression of discontent and revolt.

The heart of bin Laden's global network is Saudi Arabia, which explains why the United States has gotten far less cooperation from that nation during its war in Afghanistan than it desired. The Saudi rulers know that if the thousands of discontented young men who go to fight jihads in foreign lands stay at home instead, many are likely to challenge their authority. In a word, Saudi Arabia has exported potential trouble. The regime there knows that if it gives the United States everything it asks for, there is a serious risk of political turmoil, and it may even be overthrown in the name of Islam. But bin Laden's vision is not confined to one nation but encompasses the entire Islamic world, and even if there is not the remotest chance that his vague theocratic notions for it will be realized, al-Qaeda interacts with existing instabilities and grievances and may destabilize various Muslim nations. For bin Laden's primitivist Islamic appeals are very powerful, especially among the young, and many clerics strongly support his antiforeign rhetoric. He has shown this already in Afghanistan; but there are much more important places, where ignorance, injustice, and hunger have created a heady symbiosis of discontent and potential rebellion where the ground is already fertile.

Should Saudi Arabia undergo an Islamic revolution such as bin Laden and those who share his beliefs desire, or should the unstable society produce some fundamental changes that challenge the anachronistic political and social order that has existed there for over two centuries, then the strategic and economic consequences for the United States will be enormous. Afghanistan's destiny, by comparison, will be of minor consequence. Sooner or later, it is likely to happen.

Meanwhile, the United States' political strategy of isolating and imposing sanctions on Iraq, Libya, and Iran because of their alleged links with terrorism has greatly reduced its access to oil, which it will have to import in ever larger quantities. Germany, France, and Italy, among others, have actively sought to buy oil from these nations, and Russia will sell Iran billions of dollars of arms and finish a giant nuclear power plant there. Iran alone has the world's fifth largest proven oil reserves, and it is especially enticing. At the same time, of course, these NATO members joined the American war against terrorism, which Washington has cast in broad terms to include Iraq, Libya, and Iran among those states that encourage terrorism. Largely because of the pro-Israel lobby in Congress, the United States has a law that can even impose penalties on any foreign company that invests more than $20 million in Iran or Libya, but important American oil firms regard these gestures as counterproductive aids to French and other rivals for the control of oil supplies. Vice President Dick Cheney, when he headed the giant oil services company Halliburton, was opposed to sanctions against Iran, and legal restrictions are hardly enforced, if at all.

The emergence of Islamic fundamentalism reflects in part the failure of America's efforts in the Middle East. While its position on Israel is the single most important error it made and the one that even its closest friends in the region argue was the origin of terrorism and anti-Americanism, there were also other causes for hostility toward the United States. These I have only outlined in this chapter. The Bush administration acknowledged that strong U.S. support for Israel has alienated even its conservative friends in the area, above all the Saudis, and has surely made it far more difficult to gain support from Muslim countries for the coalition it alleged it wished to build to fight in Afghanistan and eradicate "terrorism" globally. Even before September 11 the administration acknowledged that America's bias in favor of Israel was harming it. But it is too late for the United States to undo the compounded policy errors of successive administrations over the past forty years. If it can override the powerful pro-Israel bloc in the Senate and House, which is most doubtful, it may even seek to do so by favoring a Palestinian state or attempting to impose a peace settlement on both sides. But it is unlikely to succeed. Israel is now far too strong militarily and politically, and its leaders will make few, if any, of the essential real concessions that will be required. Arafat is far too weak and his hold on the Palestinian people is too contested. Neither Israel's political leaders nor Arafat will commit political suicide among their domestic political constituencies and try to achieve a genuine peace settlement. Both sides are unwilling and unable to act rationally, and it is scarcely a promising situation.

But there are other reasons besides Israel for the strategic and policy impasse the United States now confronts. All of its policies in the Middle East have collectively produced a disaster which now not only threatens to destabilize nations crucial to its interests but—and this is infinitely more important—endangers its very security at home and world peace. It made many errors elsewhere, of course, but by encouraging fundamentalist Islam and traditionalism as an alternative to nationalism, and then profoundly alienating the reactionary and repressive regimes that fostered them, the United States has now become involved in a conflict which—temporary military successes notwithstanding—it will only lose. Opinion in the Arab world has been overwhelmingly critical of the United States' war in Afghanistan, which the Arab media accurately portray as a form of bullying terrorism and political adventurism quite independent of the Taliban and bin Laden. The opportunism that the United States rationalized as anticommunism, which led it to enthusiastically support oppressive regimes, has now created a permanent crisis extending over the Islamic arc reaching from the Mediterranean to South Asia.

It is a crisis the United States will confront in the decades to come.

3

THE TRAP:
AFGHANISTAN AND THE UNITED STATES

The United States first laid a trap in Afghanistan for the Russians, but now it too has fallen into it—the consequence of the unlimited ambition of its foreign policy. It is a consummate irony that the very same fighters who used American funds and arms to defeat the Soviets during the 1980s led the most important opposition to the United States after the mid-1990s, and that many of the Afghan warlords whom the Pentagon supported with air cover, money, and supplies in the fall of 2001 once fought on the Soviet side. The Russians may ultimately gain the most from the war that the Bush administration fought in Afghanistan in 2001.

Afghanistan: The Roots of Crisis

One monarch, Zahir Shah, ruled Afghanistan for forty years, until July 1973, when his cousin, Muhammad Daoud, overthrew him. Their power was based on the Pashtuns, who constitute about 40 percent of the population, but in reality Afghanistan remained highly decentralized, with warlords, tribal chiefs, and the like ruling most of it. The royal family ruled Kabul ineffectually—the U.S. embassy there in May 1972 believed that a "creeping crisis" was occurring—but its power outside that atypical, isolated city was minimal and frequently nonexistent.[1] Diplomatically the country was essentially neutral, and therefore of slight interest to the great powers. Unlike the majority of the population, neither Zahir nor his cousin were Islamic fundamentalists. Daoud was an opportunist and interested principally in power, and by 1975 he had banned all opposition parties. Like his dispossessed cousin he did not recognize the borders with Pakistan. Despite his authoritarianism, he also pretended to be a modernizer, and fundamentalists called his reforms atheistic. He flirted with annexing the very large Pashtun region of Pakistan—containing about 15 percent of Pakistan's population—and creating a vaguely defined new state, "Pashtunistan," modeled after Bangladesh. Naturally, Pakistan feared him and aided his Islamic enemies to keep him preoccupied; an insurgency existed. He was closest to Iran, then ruled by the shah, and the United States approved of him. But Daoud was killed in April 1978, and a gravely divided Communist Party took over an area no greater than Daoud himself had ruled.

Left to its own devices it is highly probable that this utterly fractured entity, which began purging its own ranks ruthlessly, would have lost power very quickly. This was all the more likely because the Communist regime almost immediately sought to give women equal rights and introduce land reform. As a result, it had to confront diverse bloody rebellions—which Iran and Pakistan aided. When Islamic fundamentalists took power in Iran in January 1979, Afghanistan's geopolitical importance increased greatly. It was at this point that both the Soviet Union and the United States began to pay attention to what had been a relatively unimportant country. Indeed, from this time onward Afghanistan's acute internal divisions were greatly exacerbated by its neighbors and the United States supporting contending parties, and this internationalization of an already highly fractious situation has continued since then.

At the end of March 1979 senior American officials carefully contemplated whether "there was value in keeping the Afghan insurgency going, 'sucking the Soviets into a Vietnamese quagmire.'" On July 3 President Carter signed a directive authorizing secret aid to the opponents of the pro-Soviet regime, and as Zbigniew Brzezinski, his national security adviser, correctly recalled in 1998, the explicit aim was "to induce a Soviet military intervention. . . . I wrote to President Carter: We now have the opportunity of giving to the USSR its Vietnam war." [2]

The American objective was to see the Soviet Union mauled, not to help the Afghans. It was to bait the Russians, and a bloody war on Afghan soil was only a means to this end. There was also the added attraction that Soviet intervention would "inflame Moslem opinion against them in many countries." [3] Peace, on the contrary, was never a goal save until the Soviets were mauled; that the Afghans had to pay an immense human price in the process was scarcely a consideration. This fact was crucial.

The Russians fell into the trap, encouraged by the pleas of their comrades in Kabul, whom they regarded as consummately irresponsible and unlikely to last much longer. At first they were determined not to send troops, but they also feared that the United States would replace the electronic intelligence listening posts it had just lost in Iran with new installations in Afghanistan; the CIA had begun to survey sites there—and the Soviets knew it. In late October 1979 they began preparations to invade, but it was not until December 24 that they actually began to send the first of about one hundred thousand soldiers. Moreover, the fall of the shah to fundamentalists and the political destabilization of the entire region made what happened in Afghanistan more important to them.[4] Ostensibly, the Carter Doctrine was proclaimed the following month with this invasion in mind, but the Soviets only did what the United States both desired and expected.

Covert aid to the mujahideen was relatively modest until 1984, when the Pakistanis and Saudis convinced the United States that the Soviets could be not just bled but defeated. In all, the CIA supplied the Afghan rebels with $3 billion in military aid over the next decade, and the Saudis contributed at least $2 billion. Pakistan's intelligence was in charge of actually distributing this vast flow, which was the largest American operation of this sort in history, costing as much as all its many other covert operations during that decade combined. Islamic fundamentalists and Pashtuns received most of this aid because Pakistan's interest in the war's outcome was primordial—it wanted not just anticommunists to win but those who accepted both the existing borders and its primary influence over internal political affairs in a nation sharing a fifteen-hundred-mile frontier with it. Its political and theological partiality, and that of the Saudis, was often ruthless. Iran supported tribes hostile to both the Soviets and Pashtuns.

Most of the senior Taliban leaders, as well as bin Laden and many of his chief aides, gained their formidable experience in the anti-Soviet campaign funded by the United States and

Saudi Arabia. At least fifteen thousand and as many as thirty thousand foreign fighters joined the mujahideen, and the chief of Saudi intelligence chose bin Laden as the key leader of the important "Arab brigade" among them. The Saudi regime saw Afghanistan as a useful place to send its own potential opponents, thereby neutralizing them. Bin Laden's tasks included establishing recruiting offices in thirty-five countries—there were thirty offices in American cities alone. This large network later became crucial when he created al-Qaeda in 1989 and established training camps in Afghanistan, the Philippines, Sudan, and Somalia. Religion was the principal reason foreigners volunteered; initially they were fighting a jihad against communism, but eventually they evolved into an international brigade, believers in a distinctive synthesis of extreme Islamicism and violence that pitted them after 1989 against the existing Muslim states—and the United States. They were crucial in establishing extremist Islamic movements in a number of nations, and many were incubated in Afghanistan. Thousands—about two thousand in Bosnia alone—subsequently fought in Chechnya, Algeria, Somalia, Kosovo, the Philippines, and elsewhere. Some remained in Afghanistan, joined later by others, as the backbone of the Taliban regime. Ultimately, al-Qaeda may have trained and indoctrinated up to seventy thousand potential fighters—and terrorists—and created cells in at least fifty countries. At the inception, to repeat a crucial point, they were anti–Soviet freedom fighters, financed with U.S. and Saudi money.[5]

Around 15,000 Soviet troops were killed and many more were wounded; a total of 620,000 served there. In May 1988 the Soviet Union admitted defeat, and it withdrew its troops over the next ten months. It had been the Soviets' Vietnam, helping to bring down communism in Russia, and it ended exactly as the United States had planned it a decade earlier.

The Americans, their grandiose goals attained, immediately withdrew their money, resources, and interest. "It was a great victory," the former director of the CIA noted in his memoir published in 1996. "Now the Afghans could resume fighting among themselves—and hardly anyone cared."[6] In 1990 the U.S. Congress imposed sanctions on Pakistan because it was developing nuclear weapons, though it had begun to do so much earlier.

About one million Afghans died during this war—some because of Soviet bombs and artillery, many from hunger, others caught in battles—and the nation was left in chaos. Tribes and factions were still locked in warfare. Millions were refugees, mainly in Pakistan, but Iran claimed to have nearly two million of them. Pakistan decided to end this anarchy, and it was instrumental in creating and funding the Taliban, many of whom had been trained in religious schools in Pakistan. Among other things, the building of a gas pipeline from Central Asia to energy-poor Pakistan required a unified Afghanistan. In 1996 the Taliban took over most of the country and created some semblance of order, which is why many Afghans supported them; but they also imposed a strict Islamic fundamentalism that shocked the world.

So the trap the Americans had set for the Soviets eventually caught them also—very badly. It was but one more confirmation of the fact that once wars begin, no one can predict their consequences, and that the wisest course every nation should follow—the United States included—is to avoid mixing in the affairs of other places.

Alliances and Coalitions: America's Dilemmas

The 1999 war in Kosovo taught the United States a lesson it does not wish to repeat. A great deal went badly, and there were many unpleasant surprises. President Clinton thought the bombing might "be over within a couple of days" once Slobodan Milosevic saw the alliance was united.[7] The air war lasted seventy-eight days. The Pentagon's answer to a world of increasing political complexity was high-technology warfare with overwhelming firepower. Its faith was shared by those in power—despite the fact that the United States had lost its two most ambitious wars since 1945 against enemies who understood that decentralization made bombing and technology far less effective. Strategic air power—B-52s and B-1s—was used in ways it was not designed for, and bombing caused many people to rally to Milosevic for purely patriotic reasons. Tactical aviation was often inaccurate and killed many innocent people.

The Kosovo war, NATO's first encounter with real combat, transformed it from being a defensive alliance, essentially against the USSR, into an offensive coalition. While the new NATO projected U.S. power and ambitions into Eastern Europe as never before, it also involved a frustrating, time-consuming need to consult the organization's nineteen members about innumerable questions, targets above all. As the Pentagon later admitted, "gaining consensus among 19 democratic nations is not easy and can only be achieved through discussion and compromise."[8] America's political and military leaders resolved never to fight wars this way—which means that NATO as presently organized now has a much smaller role in their military planning. Indeed, for practical purposes NATO has been greatly expanded and yet become unimportant to the United States. It is being marginalized, and Washington will call upon it only if America wants to use it on America's own terms—which was definitely not the case in Afghanistan.

What the United States refused to admit was that the Pentagon itself was racked by disagreements, ranging from tactical decisions to fundamental issues such as whether the United States should be tied up in the Balkans in the first place. Many senior officers believed that the Persian Gulf and Korea were too important to get distracted in Yugoslavia, for these were the only places where they were prepared to fight effectively. What they did not say is that they were also slaves to plans, that world politics could not be predicted, and that their planning was largely meaningless.

The United States has fought its war against the Taliban without NATO's encumbering presence, even though many alliance members were eager to join the effort and resented their exclusion. The Germans and French are strongly opposed to giving the Americans carte blanche to continue fighting elsewhere. For Washington, alliances are constraints, and after the Kosovo war it really feels that the fewer it has, the better. It still pays obeisance to them, of course, but principally as a means of controlling other nations. In Afghanistan it simply defined for its European allies what they could do—or not do—on a take-it or leave-it basis.

Once it embarked on an air war over Yugoslavia, the United States was motivated not only by its ambitions to lead an expanded NATO but especially by the "credibility" of its military power. This obsession with credibility could only entangle its European allies in protracted wars that are not in their interests, since what is also at stake for the United States is the limits of its arms and the consequences of its being defeated or even stalemated. Such reasoning caused it to make the initial political goals of its interventions secondary, or even to forget them. In this process its increasing reliance on air power inevitably required it to strike civilian targets and populations. At no time has the United States entered a war aware of the time, material, and tragic human costs it would have to pay or demand of others.

This was shown when the United States accepted the high risk of politically destabilizing the entire region, which was a direct outcome of supporting and arming the Kosovo Liberation Army—Muslim fanatics, closely tied to bin Laden, whom the State Department in 1998 had listed as terrorists. This mode of operation began in Bosnia, notwithstanding some reticence in Washington about such marriages of convenience. This approach was the logical outgrowth of placing a much higher premium on a quick military victory and destroying targets than on attaining political results that were far more compatible with a durable peace. This practice of working with politically highly dubious elements and drug merchants is now being repeated again in Afghanistan.

The war in Yugoslavia raised again the open and potentially highly destabilizing question of Russia's future relations with Europe. While NATO agreed not to consider expansion until 2002, Slovenia, Romania, and Bulgaria were very useful allies during this conflict, and they are likely to be admitted to NATO—threatening to create a de facto cordon sanitaire on Russia's borders and revising European geopolitics fundamentally. September 11 seemed to change a great deal in Russian-

American relations because Russia's cooperation was important to the war effort. But as soon as Washington's incentives disappeared, so too did its relatively conciliatory stance—above all on its 1972 missile treaty with Russia. Meanwhile, NATO is confused and disunited about how it should treat Russia—giving the United States additional incentives to turn the alliance into a largely ceremonial organization which has no important role. Russia's economic problems will cause it to accept realities imposed upon it, but it will not like many of them, and it remains a military superpower.

The Kosovo war also brought to a head the no less worrisome problem of Europe's future military structure, and especially Germany's role in it. There is a whole range of disagreements between Washington and its nominal European allies: for example, whether a projected and expanded European Union military force—which the United States nominally favors—will be independent of NATO (and an American veto!), or Europe's dislike of a missile defense system, which many nations as early as 1999 regarded as a destabilizing example of Washington's growing unilateralism. This projected missile shield and the U.S. Senate's rejection of a test ban treaty caused many important Europeans to conclude that the Americans did not want arms control—and preferred overwhelming military superiority. The Clinton administration had already indicated that "NATO could become a relic" if Europe ended the interminable and highly ambivalent debate and went ahead to create a military force parallel rather than subordinate to NATO's.[9] The Bush administration takes exactly the same position.

Germany is the crux of this issue, and it remains undecided about what its future military role will be—either in Europe or outside of it. Both the British and French fear that its military power could equal its dominant economic role in Europe, but Germany is attempting to define a role for itself and is no longer willing to remain passive. The Gerhard Schroeder government supported the war in Kosovo although only a small proportion of Germans were for sending troops there, and it has taken the military lead in Macedonia; but a majority favor the American "war on terrorism," and so the government offered four thousand men for use in the war. Germany has yet to determine the full extent of its future course, save that it wishes considerably greater prominence in European and world affairs; its reflections may appear ambiguous, but it is moving in the direction of assuming a far larger role than it has until now and translating its industrial into military power. The outcome of this change is of fundamental consequence to all of its neighbors—with whom it has fought two wars in the past century—and to the United States as well.

These basic issues, which have immense implications for Europe's future, can easily fracture its post-1945 alliances and friendships. The cold war is dead, but what will replace it? The dissolution of the USSR has destroyed the raison d'être of NATO and forty years of alliances, and Europe itself is changing rapidly both diplomatically and economically. Today, nothing is settled.

Alliances, Coalitions, Confusion

It is this context that makes the Bush administration's euphoria over new alliances and coalitions mere quixotic and insincere rhetoric, and its position obfuscates historic realities that will not disappear easily, much less with meaningless gestures. Ad hoc proposals will not be taken seriously, nor should they be, because the issues and risks involved in alliances between states are far too important to be arranged hastily and carelessly. Indeed, alliances in the past have been sources of grave tension and have caused nations to go to war when they should not have. World War I is the best example.

It is inaccurate to call America's leaders duplicitous, because that implies they really know where they want to go. They do not, and whether one describes their state of mind after the end of the cold war as being in transition or confused is less important than the fact that it is folly for any nation to place its confidence in America. What is certain is that until September 11 the Bush administration had embarked on a unilateralist course, one that dismissed treaties and distressed many of its allies, only to completely reverse itself for some months; it is now returning to its unilateralism, which fits its triumphalism much better. Its traditional allies remain skeptical that it can be trusted to continue with its new "internationalism" once it believes it has won its war on terrorism.

Nothing illustrates this more than its relations with Russia, its former enemy, which is still a nuclear superpower. When the Bush administration took office it left open the eventual acceptance of Lithuanian, Latvian, and Estonian applications for membership in NATO. Then in March 2001 it expelled fifty Russian diplomats from the United States—an action intended to show that the president was committed to a new "realism" with America's former enemy. "[W]e are on a collision course" with the Russians regarding the 1972 accord on nuclear arms control, Paul Wolfowitz told the Senate in July 2001.[10]

September 11 dramatically changed this growing public hostility toward Russia, although in private many administration officials are still skeptical of Russia; but there were growing doubts within Washington's own ranks—mainly for technological reasons—regarding an antiballistic missile system's feasibility and the future of NATO. Even without the new crisis, American foreign policy was adrift in terms of both means and objectives. Its cold war assumptions were no longer relevant, but its stance accelerated the transition without ending its inherent confusions and aimlessness. Russia was only one of many exceedingly complex problems, ranging from China and Korea to Latin America, confronting it. The Bush administration immediately shifted on Russia's brutal policy toward Chechnya because the Chechnyan revolt is indeed an Islamic rebellion, and bin Laden's followers are deeply involved in it. But the United States needed Russia's cooperation, and that gave President Vladimir Putin important leverage as well as some difficult options. One of his worries is that important sectors of his military leadership oppose his concessions to the United States, but he can point out to them that Russia has won the most politically, at least for the time being, from the war the United States fought in Afghanistan.

In this situation, both Russia and the United States did a great deal of posturing, leaving noncommittal hints and making statements on crucial issues. It was a rich field on which diplomats could play their games. But we should believe nothing until much illusion is eliminated, for both insincerity and genuine confusion reign in Moscow and Washington.

The United States wanted access to Russian airspace but was denied permission to fly in warplanes. Much more important, after seeking options and finding there were none of military consequence, the United States chose to rely principally on the Northern Alliance in Afghanistan to provide the absolutely indispensable ground forces without which the Taliban would not have been driven out of cities. This the Alliance often accomplished less by fighting than by making deals with local warlords and chieftains to desert the Taliban camp. American money and weapons were passed out liberally. The Russians covertly armed major components of the Alliance after 1996 (many of whose leaders had earlier worked with the Soviets), hoping to create a buffer along its borders and prevent Islamic extremism from spreading to the now independent former Soviet republics. After September 11 they rushed the Alliance a new infusion of tanks, artillery, and other heavy equipment. If the Alliance's disparate components are oriented to any foreign nation, it is still largely Russia, which—much to Washington's displeasure—was the first permitted to establish an armed presence in Kabul, in late November of last year. Kabul's first ruler after it fell, and Afghanistan's president from 1992 to 1996, Burhanuddin Rabbani, has in recent years been a Russian client. He was also crucial in constructing the successor government—though there are countless factors to disunite it—and still wields great power. If there is political chaos in Afghanistan and the rival ethnic groups, warlords, and clans resume their traditional fighting, which began as soon as the Taliban were nearly defeated, then at least the Russians will have a buffer in the form of the Alliance—and de facto partition of what is a nation in name only.

There are very crucial disagreements between Washington and Moscow, the end of the cold war notwithstanding. Should

Russia resume selling arms to Iran, which it suspended in 1995, and build another nuclear power reactor there? Should it continue its trade with Iraq (it is by far Iraq's largest trading partner) under the UN-sanctioned oil-for-food program? The United States and Russia could not agree to alternatives to the 1972 arms treaty, but the Russians hinted they might be amenable to some changes—although what kind remained vague. Instead, at the end of 2001 the United States simply renounced the 1972 accord.

Among the multiple questions of U.S. and Russian relations are the former Soviet republics Uzbekistan and Tajikistan, and gas pipelines that may eventually run from Turkmenistan—another former Soviet republic—which possesses 30 percent of the world's known gas reserves. Uzbekistan signed a secret accord with the United States in October 2001 that will bring it up to $150 million in loans and grants and unknown security guarantees, for which America got undisclosed operational rights. For the United States, ostensibly, it was a historic precedent: "[W]e are not going to love them and leave them," a senior American said; "[b]ut it is not the kind of blood oath that we take in NATO."[11] The Uzbek government immediately began dragging its feet on things both the United States and the UN wanted done. Tajikistan was even more important as a potential staging ground for U.S. forces, but there is a risk of a resumption of a Muslim-based guerrilla struggle; there are about twenty thousand Russian troops on its soil who operate the bases. The Tajiks have to tread a fine line, and like the Uzbeks, they tied some onerous conditions to treaties. Turkmenistan, the region's most valuable prize, is strictly neutral and even refused to allow America to use its airspace for military flights. So the Pentagon chose Kyrgyzstan as the least complicated place to build a large air base capable of acting as a transport hub for the entire region. But even here the treaty between the two nations is valid for only a year at a time. The United States ended its war in Afghanistan with thirteen new bases in nine countries, and it had no presence in most of them before September 11. At least four are Islamic and unstable; it is a recipe for new resentments and potential troubles for America.

As for gas and pipelines, the Russians have gone to great pains to make certain they will have a crucial role in the lucrative business, and the United States has tried to reassure them that it will respect their legitimate interests in the region. But what this means in practice is very much an open question. Possible pipeline routes and the exceedingly complex geopolitics of the vast area still have to be resolved, and American firms may or may not heed Washington's present commitments.

Who rules Kabul is crucial to deciding these byzantine intrigues, and at the present time—to repeat an absolutely vital point—Russia seems likely to become the main political beneficiary of the war the Americans waged. Washington's only consolation may be that it avenged the September 11 attacks. But Russia's generals strongly oppose American bases and influence in a Central Asian region that was once a part of the USSR, and Putin needs their support. They have been important in the past, and whether Putin has undermined his power is just another intangible in the very complex global geopolitical picture that the American war on terrorism has created. China too is suspicious of America's new role in Central Asia.

Meanwhile, the United States is getting thoroughly entangled in an area full of great promise and grave problems.

Uzbekistan's ruling regime is the most oppressive in the region. Its jails are full of President Islam Karimov's quite diverse enemies, which include an Islamic insurgency whose militants may number as many as twenty thousand. Turkmenistan is also run by a dictator. In fact, every one of the five former Soviet republics suffers from varying degrees of corruption, poverty, and authoritarianism—and thus are fertile breeding grounds for exactly the sort of Islamic extremism that Washington says it now seeks to extirpate. At the beginning of 2002 the Bush administration let it be known that human rights would no longer be a consideration in its relations with these nations.

How the United States becomes more directly involved in the vast Central Asian area impinges directly on its relations with Russia—which has immense geopolitical and economic interests involved. Where all this leads depends on many considerations, including the war in Afghanistan and, above all, the war's political aftermath in the coming years. At this point we can realistically dread the worst-case scenarios. There are many seeds here for future conflicts over the course of the next decades.

Destabilizing the Islamic World

Communism's virtual disappearance caused the geopolitical and strategic factors that produced alliances and coalitions after 1947 to decline and lose their justifications everywhere, but new ones have been more difficult to make. The situation in the entire Islamic world is too unstable, the outcome of the changes that are occurring within it unknowable. But America's war in Afghanistan further destabilized Pakistan and weakened the

ruling family in Saudi Arabia, making the long-term consequences of the conflict in Afghanistan pale in importance. Any
upheavals in either of these two crucial nations are likely to
bring to power men essentially sympathetic to one or another
brand of Islamic fundamentalism. To win the war militarily but
lose it politically would be a disaster for the United States, one
it is very likely going to have to confront soon.

There are a number of ways Pakistan could be shaken to its
core. Washington was aware of these dangers but decided to
play a perilous game with high risks, and now there is a strong
chance it will see the worst case realized. Some of these issues
are very old, involving Pakistan's fundamental interest in seeing
a friendly regime rule its northern neighbor, and will continue
in the future regardless of whether or not General Pervez
Musharraf continues to rule. Until the fighting was resolved Pakistan had much more leverage in dealing with the United
States, but the moment the fighting ended, most of that leverage
was lost. Pakistani public sentiment was from the inception
hostile to Musharraf's alliance with America. In mid-October
2001, public opinion was 87 percent opposed to the U.S. attacks, and nearly two-thirds were pro-Taliban. Thousands of
Pakistani men—Pashtuns—have gone to Afghanistan in recent
years to fight for the Taliban. Pakistan has always been a politically fragile partner in whatever the United States chooses to
label its relationship. Basing U.S. strategy in the region on Pakistan was folly, for the worst of all worlds is to destabilize it, leading to Islamic fundamentalists taking power—for the nation to
be "Talibanised," as one former Pakistani senior official put it.[12]

No one could predict the sequence of events that brought
India and Pakistan at the end of 2001 to the awesome brink of

their fourth war since 1947—with each state now possessing nuclear weapons. In October 2001 Pakistan-supported Kashmiri terrorists assaulted the parliament in Indian-controlled Srinagar in Kashmir and killed thirty-eight people. Then on December 13 they attacked India's parliament in Delhi itself, resulting in fourteen deaths. Both India and Pakistan readied their nuclear bombs while intensive fighting with conventional weapons erupted along the cease-fire line in Kashmir, a line which was established in this largely Muslim province in 1948 and gives India about two-thirds of the disputed territory. This unforeseen event was a windfall for India, which chose to attempt finally to resolve the principal dispute that has produced a guerrilla war which has caused at least thirty-three thousand deaths and blighted relations between the two states for over a half century. Its military mobilization was the largest in its history, and it showed no readiness to back away from war. Indeed, politically, the Indian government could not do so easily without Pakistan making significant concessions.

The frightening Indian-Pakistani confrontation revealed that U.S. actions have destabilized the entire precarious South Asian geopolitical balance, and this is of far greater consequence over the long term than what happens in Afghanistan. Pakistan has lost what it terms "strategic depth" in Afghanistan, leaving it more vulnerable than ever to Indian demands that Pakistan end its claims on Indian-controlled Kashmir and cease supporting guerrillas there.

Washington officials sought to court both Pakistan and India. The Indians correctly pointed out that the Taliban regime and al-Qaeda trained many of the separatist guerrillas in Indian-held Kashmir; over half of those killed there since 2000 are of foreign nationality—mainly Pakistanis but also Arabs, some of whom gained experience while fighting Soviet troops. Pakistan became the principal source of support for these guerrillas after 1990; it calls them freedom fighters, but many are Islamic extremists recruited by pro-Taliban Islamic groups in Pakistan and now largely controlled by a branch of Pakistan's intelligence. No one, Musharraf made clear in his ostensible peace overture to India at the beginning of 2002, would be handed over to foreign authorities, not even those involved in the attack on India's parliament. But at the beginning of 2002 he did take steps to placate India: he closed training camps for Kashmiri guerrillas in Pakistan, outlawed five "extremist" organizations supporting them, detained about two thousand people (he released a large majority in March), and said he would impose controls over the Islamic schools that are the hotbed from which the Taliban emerged. These organizations trained at least five thousand men. Now they are likely to go underground, becoming potentially even more dangerous. That they represent a relatively small minority is less consequential than their determination. India is interested in deeds, not words, and certainly did not demobilize the vast armies it had stationed on Pakistan's borders. By breaking with Islamic extremists, as India and Washington demand he do as part of the war on terrorism, Musharraf also risks undermining his Kashmir policy and the support of the military.

Musharraf simply cannot afford to turn the Islamicists and their allies in the military against him. So in January 2002, even when on the brink of war with India over Kashmir, he stated that he would not cut Pakistani aid to those indigenous Kashmiris fighting India's control of the disputed province. He wished to prevent another war with India, but he also vaguely declared that Pakistan was as committed to the Kashmir cause as ever. Whether he has the power or will to end support to the Pakistan-based terrorists who are India's principal foes in Kashmir is still an open question. There is an independent dynamic in Kashmir and too many unpredictable factors to assume that the contentious problems there will be settled soon.

These questions may be answered by the time this book appears in print. If not, they will endure, and reemerge sooner or later. Meanwhile there will be acute, frightening tension between two nations that have often fought each other. What the crisis does confirm, regardless of any short-term settlements that may be reached, is that any dispute between nuclear powers can threaten the peace and stability of entire regions, and that as more nations acquire these weapons, the world will become even more dangerous—hence rational political solutions, compromises, and arms control become more imperative.

Pakistan was much more important than India to the United States only as long as the United States fought in Afghanistan, but its tradition of coups—which is how General Musharraf came to power in October 1999—makes Pakistan all the more unstable and worrisome to the Bush administration. The net effect of Washington's actions was to strengthen Musharraf's position and at the beginning of 2002 he promised to remain president for five more years, perhaps turning the elections scheduled for October 2002 into a referendum to legitimize his authority. But his readiness to alienate the Islamic militants who have been a pillar of military-dominated regimes for decades in reality makes him weaker than ever. Meanwhile, the United

States sought to reassure India, which rightly believed that it had tilted to Pakistan. The United States now confronts a geopolitical dilemma in South Asia that it cannot solve.

Its relations with India and the Kashmir question are of primordial importance to Pakistan, and control of its nuclear arsenal of twenty to fifty warheads and the missiles to deliver them is linked to Pakistan's security. It also has a very great security interest in seeing a friendly Afghanistan on its long northern border—which means Pashtuns must control it. The Northern Alliance has few Pashtuns in its ranks, and its quick military triumph in the cities during the first weeks of the war was due wholly to the support of American air power, just as aviation was quickly effective only because the Alliance's troops forced the Taliban to concentrate their soldiers. The Bush administration was unwilling to send large numbers of soldiers or risk the casualties that fighting in cities entails, and so Pakistan's interest in having Pashtuns play an important role in the future was ignored. Defense Secretary Rumsfeld has admitted that this "cooperative effort" was decisive and that the Alliance played the role of proxies for American ground forces; in addition to air power, the Americans supplied the Alliance with food, money to buy warlords' fealties, and munitions.[13] One by-product was that many Taliban and al-Qaeda leaders—including probably bin Laden himself—were able to bargain or buy their escapes from their pragmatic Afghan opponents, thereby depriving the United States of the total elimination of its enemies which was one of its principal war aims. Much to the United States' dismay some captured senior Taliban military as well as civil officials were almost immediately allowed to go free. When the Taliban regime began to capsize late in 2001, the Bush administration was compelled to allow Pakistan secretly to airlift out many hundreds of its volunteers who had gone to fight in Afghanistan, including officers and intelligence operatives on assignment. An unknown number of Taliban and al-Qaeda members escaped this way. The United States agreed reluctantly only because the alternative was to strengthen Musharraf's Islamic opponents within the military and intelligence, perhaps leading to his overthrow, and it was unwilling to take this risk. The United States did not want Alliance forces to enter Kabul, but it knew that there was not the slightest reason to assume that the warlords constituting it would obey America. But the Alliance openly detests Pakistan, which created and backed the Taliban and allowed it to keep its embassy open long after the war began. Among the first actions of the new regime in Kabul was to send its foreign minister to Delhi.

Pakistan's security interests have now been imperiled, and its enemies are again on its borders; Afghanistan is very likely to be Pakistan's fractious, unstable neighbor. Musharraf not only lost his gamble there, he lost it very badly. "A strategic debacle," a "quagmire," is how senior Pakistanis described the situation at the end of November 2001, even before the crisis with India erupted.[14] If the remnants of the Taliban or Pashtuns fight whatever government emerges in the north, then Pakistan will be under great pressure to get involved in some way, ranging from opening its borders to supplying the regime's opponents. It has often done so in the past.

Pakistan's nuclear arsenal falling into the hands of Islamic extremists is a possibility, however remote, and it will exist as long a significant part of the military and intelligence—estimates run between 25 and 30 percent—are strong Islamicists. This risk is inherent in the proliferation of nuclear weapons, whatever the country, and while the Pakistanis assure everyone that they have firm control over their bombs, they also briefly detained several of their leading nuclear scientists who are Islamic fundamentalists and friendly to the Taliban. The situation in South Asia is much more dangerous than ever before. But that is the way the world has become in the twenty-first century.

Pakistan's instability is very much linked to the power its intelligence service, Inter-Services Intelligence (ISI), amassed while working as the CIA's conduit to the mujahideen in the 1980s. Dismissing the head of the agency at the beginning of October 2001 was a gesture only; most of its members are hostile to the U.S. war because the political turmoil which followed the Soviet defeat there was the reason the Pashtun-based Taliban came to power in 1996 with the ISI's help. Pakistan fears, with ample justification, that the Americans will abandon the region once they win militarily, as they did in 1989, and that it will again have to confront a political vacuum and chaos to the north. The Pashtuns—along with the three million Afghan refugees—are the most important ethnic group within Pakistan along the long border with Afghanistan, and this and ISI connivance explain not only why the Taliban received a considerable traffic of food and vital materials from Pakistan during October and November of 2001 but why Washington believed the ISI helped al-Qaeda and Taliban fighters to escape once the regime had been defeated. The entire region on both sides is essentially a Pashtun domain, and some thousands of them—perhaps more—crossed the border to join the Taliban before they were defeated. Now that the Taliban have lost, at least in the cities, Musharraf confronts opposition from these people, and it will add to his worries or even threaten his rule. Musharraf may purge some Islamic hard-liners and even attempt to establish relations with whatever powers exist in Afghanistan, but the basic geopolitical shift against Pakistan's historic interests since the fall of 2001, first in Afghanistan and then in Kashmir and in its relations with India, is a reality that will gravely haunt—and undermine—his government. Pakistan cannot militarily confront tension along both its northern and southern borders at the same time. There are many in the intelligence service and the military who regard the outcome of his policies as a disaster.

The ISI continues to be crucial in Pakistani politics. General Musharraf would not have come to power in a coup in October 1999 without the help of the ISI head, whom he nevertheless fired in October 2001. And more than ever, the crisis in relations with India means that Musharraf needs as wide a base of support as possible, including the Islamic groups as well as secular democrats. Should he be replaced one way or another, then who or what would follow him is an open question, but it might include, in whole or in part, the small but very militant Islamic fundamentalists. That nuclear weapons would fall into their hands is speculation, but it is much more likely this way than any other—and that would greatly increase the dangers in South Asia. Either way, should Musharraf be overthrown because he has been too close to the United States, then Pakistan would be far more hostile to America's role and interests in the region.

Unfortunately for Musharraf, the United States was in neither a position nor a mood to help him install friends of Pakistan in Kabul when the war ended. Musharraf and the ISI badly wanted the bombing to be of very short duration, lest the Pakistani population's sympathies with the Taliban continue to intensify with their suffering. The United States did not press Pakistan for the optimum use of its bases for fear of creating a potentially destabilizing public backlash. It did get three bases in isolated Baluchistan from which several thousand of its Special Forces operated; however, it relied upon aircraft carriers as much as possible. There were important protests, but the regime could cope with them. When the Northern Alliance won in Afghanistan, Pashtuns there received temporary and symbolic posts only—which probably means a return of the instability that racked the nation for over a decade. The Alliance comprises a disparate, fractious united front of warlords from various ethnic minorities for whom, to quote Donald Rumsfeld, fighting "is a way of life." Some have switched sides—often—in return for money or promises. Fighting between them began as soon as the Taliban were defeated in most of the country. Without a durable political agreement that produces stability, Alliance military successes pose formidable risks that American officials are well aware of—and such an agreement has eluded the ethnically deeply divided nation for over a decade. It was the chaos that the Alliance's factions produced after 1990, especially in the cities, "which gave rise," to quote Colin Powell, "to the Taliban." [15]

This is a major reason why, with the war largely won militarily, Washington has sought to avoid any major role in resolving Afghanistan's internecine factional strife—"nation building," as it is called. It has assigned the United Nations complete responsibility for attempting to establish a coalition government. Politically it knows the cause is likely to be lost—indeed, that

Russia and Iran may become the key players in determining events there, even if Pakistan disapproves of ethnic groups hostile to it taking regional or national power. Political disorder, even chaos, is more than likely to be the eventual outcome of its devastating bombing on behalf of the Northern Alliance's ground forces. The other reason for the United States' non-involvement is that war there was wholly in response to the September 11 events. The United States wanted to maintain its credibility, which required a war in which revenge was its principal goal. Its political and military priorities remain elsewhere. In a word, the United States will succeed militarily but fail politically.

With good cause, the Pakistanis regard the Alliance as agents of Russia and Iran who will allow the return of anarchy and atrocities, as they did in the early 1990s. The Northern Alliance, with equally valid reasons, considers the Taliban to be a Pakistani creation, and the one thing that unites it is its hatred of Pakistan and its efforts to create a puppet regime on its border.

The United States has tried to do the best it can with what it has. Politically it has made no progress in finding political or ethnic elements with whom Pakistan can live. At the same time, it badly needed the few bases the Pakistanis gave them and whatever intelligence the ISI provided. The ISI gave far less information than the Pentagon desired or needed, and it was accused of being pro-Taliban. Militarily the United States greatly aided the Northern Alliance, over which it had little if any control, because it did not find alternatives to it, despite intensive efforts to do so. The United States' unwillingness to put significant numbers of ground troops in the country before the Alliance's disparate components entered and took charge of the major cities strained America's relations with Pakistan as never before—perhaps to the breaking point. Politically, the Alliance is anathema in most of the country, and likely to drive at least some Pashtuns who dislike the Taliban to make common cause with what is left of them. "I think he's got one of the toughest jobs in the world right now," Rumsfeld summed up Musharraf's position in mid-November.[16] Musharraf could not or did not stop many Taliban and their Arab fighters from crossing to safety into Pakistan, and over five thousand escaped this way. When the crisis with India began in mid-December he withdrew the large majority of regular troops sent to the border region. But although Musharraf's position at home was weakened, only time will tell if Pakistan has been destabilized fatally. If it has been, then America's problems will become far greater—and much more dangerous. The United States may very well be preoccupied with the fragile region for much longer than it expected or intended.

What was a tactical victory in Afghanistan will then become a strategic debacle in South Asia.

In this context, Iran has begun to play a growing and opportunistic role as the game of nations is now being played for higher stakes. It has given more arms to Shia factions within the fractious Northern Alliance, as well as money to buy them from Russia—which is mixing politics and business. Iran detested the Taliban Sunni fanaticism as an Islamic deviation and came close to war with them in 1998, when the Taliban murdered ten Iranian diplomats; but it also greatly fears a pro-American government along its borders. At the beginning of 2002 American officials accused Iran of aiding Alliance factions that are hostile to the United States and helping al-Qaeda fighters to escape its dragnet. At the same time, Iran is seeking to exploit America's predicaments by getting Washington to lift sanctions it has imposed, including on constructing pipelines across it—the most logical, cheapest route. How it plays out this heady, cynical game depends on many elements, not the least of which are Iran's real options and whether remnants of the Taliban survive the American onslaught.

Washington's precarious relations with Pakistan are matched by its problems with Saudi Arabia, which, as I explained in the preceding chapter, has become a much more unstable country due to various factors, of which America's role in the region is one of the most important. Both nations are crucial. If either, much less both, were destabilized, then the geopolitical and military problems confronting the United States would be far greater. Indeed, they would probably be insurmountable, although the Bush administration refused to admit that the United States' earlier involvement in Afghanistan had created such grave risks. The danger is that the United States will improvise a response to crises in either nation that are partly or wholly of its own making, and the form its actions might take is quite unpredictable.

Bin Laden probably has more influence and financial contacts in Saudi Arabia than in any other country. In part this is because the Saudis were so crucial in supplying money and men during the CIA-led war against the Soviets in Afghanistan, but instability in the internal political and social structure makes bin Laden's appeals resonate among younger, better-educated men—precisely the kind who flew the planes on September 11. Many consider him a heroic figure and a dedicated Muslim. The Saudis did not fully cooperate in 1996 in the United States' attempt to catch the perpetrators of the bombing that killed nineteen American servicemen; they failed to help the FBI and CIA to the extent these agencies asked regarding the nineteen men who hijacked planes on September 11, all of whom had Saudi passports; and they have not clamped down on the extensive financial assets of al-Qaeda and bin Laden. They have arrested some bin Laden supporters but none linked to the September 11 events.

Saudi Arabia's rulers have not staked their own future on the U.S. war in Afghanistan. While they have agreed to some of the demands that American officials have presented, essentially they have been disingenuous with everyone and tried to keep both the Americans and irate Saudis at bay. After prominent Muslim clerics in mid-October urged Muslims to wage a jihad against Americans within the kingdom and came close to identifying the royal family as apostates, the regime declared its unequivocal opposition to spreading the war to any other Arab country, namely Iraq, and even declared that it would side with them. American officials claimed that they were utilizing the ultra-modern Saudi air bases as they desired, but other than using its command and coordination equipment, American planes have not flown from there to bomb Afghanistan. The Saudis have also declared publicly that they will not allow the bases to be used in a renewed full-scale war against Iraq, even in self-defense. The exact facts will be known in due course, because it is quite possible that Saudi disclaimers are for their public's consumption only; meanwhile, Saudi public opinion, especially among the better-educated, who dislike the regime for a variety of reasons, is very hostile to the war in Afghanistan and to the United States in general. One prominent Saudi political commentator in late October declared that the United States "doesn't realize that if the government cooperates more they will jeopardize their own security."[17] But Washington knows full well that its alliance with the Saudis will work only if Iraq invades the region again, which certainly won't happen. In the meantime, the United States does not want to test already hostile Saudi public opinion. At best, the Saudi regime is a reluctant, uncooperative ally, and Washington's repeated declarations that it is very satisfied with Saudi Arabia mask a much more complex reality. It is aware of the risks if the regime is replaced; its war in Afghanistan has raised the geopolitical ante greatly, and its possible losses.

"Saudi Arabia is a pivotal country and our presence in the Gulf is strategically vital to us," as one American official succinctly put it.[18] Afghanistan has made the position of the royal dynasty, already precarious, that much more unstable. Can they weave through the incredibly complicated factors at home and abroad—in Israel especially—to survive? It is a matter not of months but of years, and the regime's future will depend on its resolving or containing the accumulation of problems it faces. Many of them are not of America's making, but collectively they interact to create a highly inflammable mixture. Were Saudi Arabia also destabilized then the United States would confront massive challenges, both in the region and its petroleum supply.

It is a fact that the war in Afghanistan has weakened the regimes in both Pakistan and Saudi Arabia, perhaps fatally, and the longer the war and its politically unstable aftermath take, the greater the risks—especially to Pakistan. These potential dangers far exceed in strategic and economic importance the issues that were involved in finding bin Laden or removing the Taliban from power.

Military Success, Political Failure

Relying heavily on the Northern Alliance's ground forces, the United States easily prevailed militarily over the Taliban. Then what? If the sequence that followed the mujahideen victory over the Soviets in 1989 is repeated, then the war will have been a political disaster. Even ignoring what may occur in Pakistan or elsewhere, there is nothing in the present constellation of forces and factors within Afghanistan to warrant confidence that America is not facing another failure there, much bigger this time because, as it did in Vietnam, it has staked its credibility.

As the wars of the past century have repeatedly shown, military victories do not bring peace. At most they produce interludes, and if the right political settlements are not attained, then violence resumes or there is political disorder. The United States has rarely, if ever, seen politics as the primary objective of making war, and it invariably seeks to win military engagements as if there is some independent reason for doing so.

In Kosovo the United States utilized the KLA, which it had earlier denounced as terrorist, because it sought to win battles, and the KLA—criminals, terrorists, and all—was deemed indispensable. American officials had ample proof of this, but they made a pact with it despite deep apprehension because they needed the KLA's help against the Serbs. In Afghanistan the United States did the same. Success in both places was measured in military terms, and that is a recipe for ultimate failure.

Afghan politics are unusually complex by any criterion, for

legally it is a nation but in reality it is divided by ethnicity, warlords and clans, cliental structures, brands of Islam, and countless other factors. The Northern Alliance reflects this disparate reality: some of its warlords, chieftains, and factions take arms and money from Iran; others receive aid from Russia, which is probably its major backer; even India has aided the Northern Alliance because of its hostility to Pakistan. Some of its most important leaders fought for the Soviet forces during the 1980s, but others fought against them, and in the fall of last year the Alliance even hired dozens of ex-Soviet soldiers to advise them. Opportunism is the rule among those who belong to it. Yet, the Pentagon, despite its initial reticence, ended by relying almost exclusively on the Alliance and provided it with guns, funds, and horrific air cover. Without it, the ground war would have confronted the United States with some overwhelming difficulties, above all the need to send in far larger numbers of troops. Instead, the Alliance became its surrogate army. Much of the Alliance's success was due to defections from the Taliban coalition. Until recently well over half of the world's opium supply came from Afghanistan; the Taliban were opposed to its cultivation and reduced it in areas it controlled to virtually nothing by 2001, but the Alliance refused to touch it—indeed, its opium revenue tripled between 1999 and 2001—and Afghanistan's opium output has returned to normal. Their position on women is as bad as the Taliban's. When the Alliance took power in most cities in the early 1990s they fought one another, and the reign of violence, terror, and chaos that ensued was the major reason the Taliban came to power. No sooner had the Northern Alliance captured Kabul last November than its factions again began fighting one another, a pattern that has subsequently been repeated elsewhere—usually for spoils and control over revenues. The only thing they have in common now is their hatred of the Taliban—and Pakistan.

Some Afghan factions in Iran regarded the Northern Alliance's willingness to work with the United States as a disgrace, and the readiness of some of its components to accept a return of the former king, a Pashtun, as foolhardy adventurism. Many of its factions and soldiers are unreliable and perfectly capable of switching sides; some of its leaders have done so in the past. As soldiers they are, at best, mediocre; fraternization and commerce between them and Taliban forces was fairly common. For many, fighting is a way of life. After failing to find options, military imperatives caused Washington to rely increasingly upon this disparate, scruffy alliance. If there is ever to be political stability in this war-torn nation, this is poor stuff to work with, and American officials have always known it. But the Alliance emerged from last fall's Bonn political negotiations on a six-month interim government as the most powerful single force.

The United States was exceedingly unhappy with the marriage of convenience it made with the Alliance, and Pakistan regards it as a sworn enemy. But to an extent that cannot be predicted, Musharraf's power is linked to alleged American assurances that the Alliance will not be permitted to reach Pakistan's border. The Alliance reciprocates by saying, quite accurately, that Pakistan put the Taliban in power and seeks to dominate the nation.

But without the agreement of both Pakistan and Iran a durable peace is very unlikely. Weaving its way through the shoals this dangerous division creates has been precariously difficult for the United States, and it is indecisive. At first it even accepted the possibility of some Taliban factions remaining in power, as Pakistan desired, but it gradually abandoned the idea. There is scarcely any constancy in its views on the future of Afghan politics. The Pentagon insisted that it would withdraw American soldiers entirely when the fighting ended and they captured or killed the Taliban and al-Qaeda leaders on their list, and while it was ready to see an international peacekeeping force in Kabul under the British and Germans, it was also reluctant to see it established before the fighting ended. To complicate the situation, the Northern Alliance opposes any extensive foreign peacekeeping force. The British were especially eager to split the Taliban's ranks, which include opportunist warlords as well as religious zealots. The important pockets of Taliban fighters who existed after they lost all the cities may very well be absorbed in this rational manner. Russia believes the Northern Alliance alone is the legitimate government, and its best-known warlord, Abdul Rashid Dostum, is an inveterate corruptionist who fought for the Soviets for nearly a decade. Iran also supports Alliance factions. At the end of 2001 Dostum also became the Pentagon's military vehicle, but he (as well as other crucial Alliance leaders) initially refused to accept the interim agreement that the anti-Taliban parties reached in Bonn last December. The result has been consummate American military opportunism in supporting the Northern Alliance, and consummate political folly and instability.

Nation building was not America's business, the Pentagon argued, and this view has prevailed because the inordinate complexity of Afghan politics makes a political settlement acceptable to all major factions virtually impossible to attain. The United States has encouraged the United Nations to deal with the disputatious factions and try to work out a political basis for a postwar coalition, but the UN personnel with the longest experience there express varying degrees of pessimism. Despite the six-month political accord some of the main Afghan factions reached in Bonn, it is much more likely that the future control of the nation, like everywhere throughout history, will depend on the results of warfare—those who control the ground will define politics—and there may even be a de facto partition. Politically, it is more than likely that Afghanistan will emerge from this war as divided as it was in the early 1990s, creating the same chaos that led to the Taliban's coming to power in the first place.

Coalitions and Strategy: Real and Imagined

The Kosovo war marked the end of NATO as one of the principal means of directly applying U.S. military power in Europe, for it was the first time that NATO had been called upon to function in an actual combat situation. Its inability to act in a timely fashion was partially an inevitable consequence of expanding its membership and extending its potential commitments until they became less and less binding, but it was largely due to the Pentagon's realization that NATO's practical encumbrances and time-consuming need to consult its members on routine military decisions made it more a liability than an asset. The war in Afghanistan is a European affair only insofar as a hitherto obscure clause in NATO's treaty makes an attack on one state an attack on all of them, but this far-fetched contingency was written with a totally different scenario in mind—the USSR was then its sole concern—and when the organization's member-ship was much smaller.

But long before September 11, the United States was deter-mined to avoid a repetition of the serious inhibitions that arose with the Kosovo war. The only question was one of timing and how the United States would escape its clear obligations while maintaining its hegemony over its other members. It wished to preserve NATO for essentially the same reasons it had created it: to restrain Europe's inclinations to create an independent military organization. If Russia reaches even a partial accord with NATO, which is being debated (with Washington often shifting its position and frustrating its nominal allies), then its original function will come to an end and it will exist in name alone. It will then be invoked solely when it suits America's purposes.

Even before the wars in the former Yugoslavia, the Pentagon was also moving away from the U.S. preoccupation with Eu-rope, a shift that the demise of communism warranted, and fo-cusing its plans far more on the Persian Gulf and especially on East Asia and China. The Bush administration came to office resolved to do less in the Balkans, essentially leaving this respon-sibility to the United States' European allies. But it also em-barked on a whole string of unilateral gestures, ranging from renouncing the Kyoto agreement to indicating that the 1972 arms control treaty with Russia was soon to become a dead let-ter. It was openly divided on such issues as relations with China and even Russia, whether to invade Iraq, and how far and fast to go with the ABM system. These internal differences have only intensified since then. America's reputation for reliability and stability, and its willingness to reshape its treaties and foreign policies as it thought expedient, were immediately called into question.

The events of September 11 compelled the United States to cease temporarily its march toward unilaterism, but it continued trying to attain its objectives in fighting terrorism without sacrificing its goal of greater freedom in its foreign and military policies. Essentially, it embarked on a public relations campaign. But this has strengthened the impression among its allies that this administration is both unstable and unreliable and has even raised some basic questions within the Pentagon and the State Department.

It told its European allies that they could offer men and equipment as individual states but that the United States would be the sole judge of how, and if, it wished to use them. NATO per se was excluded. For assorted reasons, internal politics and their image of themselves as world-class powers being the most crucial, the French, Germans, Italians, and others offered to send small numbers of forces to Afghanistan. Initially the United States did not want them, but it accepted them when it became clear that the war and especially its aftermath would take longer than the Pentagon had expected. But the United States has not consulted its allies on military matters and has treated them with indifference and disdain on political and legal questions ranging from how and where alleged terrorists are to be tried and the composition of the new regime in Afghanistan to possible expansion of the war to Iraq and elsewhere—frightening most of its important NATO allies. The United States sought Turkish forces to give its campaign a nominal Muslim complexion, but the Turks intended to extract a high economic and political price for their participation, and the public there was overwhelmingly against sending troops.

In what may be called a statement of objectives and means, a kind of doctrine, the president told Congress on September 20 that the United States would decide which state was providing "aid or a safe haven" to terrorism and would "pursue" it. But his flowery rhetoric could mean anything, and over the next months Iraq was not the only state mentioned as possibly feeling America's wrath. Sudan, Somalia, Indonesia, the Philippines, and perhaps others might also have to confront America's military power in some undefined way. On October 7 the United States sent to the United Nations a letter in which it reserved the right to take military action against countries other than Afghanistan. The British, who alone have played a substantial role in Afghanistan, immediately let it be known that they were not giving Washington carte blanche to go into Iraq or anyplace else. Indeed, after a short interlude, the British began criticizing the Americans for everything from their unwillingness to confront the Israeli-Palestinian crisis forcefully to their basic military strategy. Saudi Arabia, Egypt, and Jordan, the United States' closest allies among the Arab states, reiterated that they too wanted no war against Iraq. Instead, it sent more than six hundred soldiers to the southern Philippines, nominally to train and assist government troops against one of four Islamic guerrilla forces.

Meanwhile, the impression of American instability and confusion has been reinforced by official references to "floating coalitions," "revolving coalitions," and the like, as if nations have no enduring interests and can or will make ephemeral alliances to suit Washington's fancy to fight what it has termed "a new kind of war." [19] But this concept of a coalition is obviously superficial and can mean anything; it is merely a mask for American unilateralism—one new necessity September 11 imposed on it. This was confirmed almost immediately.

The Pentagon still confronts one fundamental problem: Before September 11 it had planned for years to move its abundant but ultimately finite resources toward the East Asia–Pacific region, which it argued remains relatively unstable but which is also of growing economic importance. Politically this was not an appealing or convincing shift in the Pentagon's emphasis, but it gave the United States tangible potential enemies—China and North Korea—and the area's great wealth justified its interest. A tremendous amount of thought went into defining a fundamental strategy that did not abandon Europe or the Gulf but was an orderly redeployment of its priorities and resources. Rumsfeld endorsed this shift in priorities and spending before September 11. Whether or not this planning reorientation is just another illusion in confronting the world's real problems is immaterial—it happened.

When the United States went pell-mell to Afghanistan, and it was a mystery what the president and some of his advisers might do next, not only its allies thought it was confused. So too did some very important people in the Pentagon, who believe that the destabilization of Pakistan would completely upset the region, with unknown but potentially calamitous consequences. Whatever the tactical gains from victory in Afghanistan, the United States' strategic problems could end up being far greater and open-ended, and it was unprepared for many if not most of them. "Our actions so far," one general said at the end of October, "show only short-term thinking." Rumsfeld imposed restraints on such talk by officers, so their criticisms were made in private; but the Pentagon's outside consultants were much more open about their misgivings. The secretary was asked about this undercurrent at the same time, ignoring entirely all of his statements on military planning the preceding nine months. "I watch people's behavior, my senior staff and the military, and I'll stop them and say look, that makes a lot of sense before September 11. How do you feel about the priority now? And yet they go along a track. We all do. We're human beings. . . . We need a lot of transformation in this building. There's no question." [20]

Since the end of the Second World War, the United States has reacted to events and crises as they occur and wherever they arise, without reflection or wisdom, and it has gone from one blunder to another. Yet it has never been more confused or dangerous, both to itself and to the world, than at the present moment.

4

THE MAKING OF AMERICAN FOREIGN POLICY: SUCCESSES, AND FAILURES

The more ambitious wars are, the greater the likelihood that they will go awry. Wars usually become nightmares that last far longer than expected, and their ultimate consequences can rarely be predicted. These monumental legacies of failure have shaped the past century profoundly and have altered decisively the existences of countless millions: destroyed their lives, driven them into exile, or traumatized what might have been the joys and cares of normal existence. Innumerable nations that embarked on vainglorious missions to use their military power to attain political goals inflicted unimaginable suffering on other countries but also on their own people, thereby condemning their own destinies: some to social and political disorder or even to revolutions, to the decline of power and prestige, and to fates that were far worse than had they done nothing. Empires have risen, but they have also fallen. The strongest argument against one nation interfering with another does not have to be deduced from any doctrine, moral or otherwise; it is found by looking honestly at the history of the past centuries.[1]

False Expectations: The Illusions of War

At the inception of the twenty-first century, even as inherited conventional wisdom has guided U.S. foreign policy, the horrors of the past are being reenacted. The same policies that in varying degrees have produced disasters for the United States are still considered the only way to relate to the continuous and growing problems of a world that was already far too complex for it to manage fifty years ago. With the rapid diffusion of ever deadlier weapons over the past decade, America is today even less able to control events; and rather than producing greater stability, the disintegration of the Communist orbit has led to a proliferation of new and usually unmanageable crises both within and between dozens of nations.

At the end of the nineteenth century there were many causes of militarism, above all in those nations that started wars, but various forms of jingoism and nationalism permeated all of the states that went to war in 1914 and again in 1939. Intellectualized doctrines of power and Darwinian biological theory were the rule rather than the exception, used to justify the colonialism of Great Britain, France, the United States, Japan, and other nations that made their foreign policies their preoccupation. Men of power everywhere, ranging from Theodore Roosevelt in the United States to most of Japan's and Germany's leaders, shared the belief that destiny had ordained them for the noble calling of armed combat. A romantic cult of action and physical fitness produced an aristocratic warrior ethos, and such notions were transnational, with morale—bravery—alleged to be the decisive element in warfare. All the political and military leaders of the belligerent nations in 1914 had read with great respect the writings of Carl von Clausewitz, a German whose pseudo-scientific theories of strategy and war gave warriors a rationale for their power; Charles Darwin, an Englishman whose notions of the survival of the fittest reinforced their ambitions; and the American Alfred Thayer Mahan, the leading theorist of naval expansion and the acquisition of foreign bases. Such romanticism was surely less important than geopolitics, domestic politics, or economics, but it persisted after 1918, when the Italians and Japanese especially shared this military consensus. What they also all held in common was the conviction that wars would be brief and fought in a strategically convenient fashion that conformed to their equipment, budgets, and priorities. In its own way, war was supposed to be rational, not catastrophic.

This persistent illusion was a grave error, but scarcely the only one. The criterion of rationality for evaluating policies that lead to war is ultimately socially conditioned, and in most nations both generals and civilians share it and produce predictably common optimistic prognoses. In every country, only a finite range of views receive a hearing in policy-making circles, and ambitious individuals fully understand the boundaries of permissible analyses. Indeed, with the growing importance of simulated war games and strategic doctrines, civilian intellectuals have often been more bellicose than officers. It is precisely because of the growing disparity between the increasingly complex realities of modern warfare and strategic estimates, and the decision-making structures that produce them, that wars increasingly create unanticipated shocks, not just military but especially political. Since the beginning of the last century, only wars have tested to their very foundations the stability of existing social systems, and communism, fascism, and Nazism would certainly not have triumphed without the events of 1914–18 to foster them.

It was precisely the optimistic illusion of wars as relatively short, even clinical events that made possible the widespread conviction that a nation's "credibility" was at stake if it refused to fight or come to the defense of its alliance members. For the nations that went to war in 1914, this readiness to use force was an article of faith; credibility was crucial to Washington's repeatedly escalating the war in Vietnam. Since such alliances have flourished, the destiny of major powers has frequently depended on the behavior and role of often fragile allied states. Coalition diplomacy and the logic of credibility have together led to wars. After 1947 the United States created the Truman Doctrine and amplified credibility to add the "domino theory" to its strategic doctrines, believing that its refusal to become involved in a relatively minor nation would lead to a succession of other and larger defeats in a region. This viewpoint was crucial in leading it into the war in Vietnam.

There have been significant differences in the ways that nations have responded to foreign policy crises, but they have also shared astonishingly similar premises and perceptions. These common assumptions made it possible for states to embark on wars, oblivious of the costs in blood, time, and property that their astonishingly adventurist and often casual policies would demand. Those whose decisions shape the world have learned very little—indeed virtually nothing—from the past century of myopia and repeated failures. We live, as never before, with the risk of yet more wars, perhaps for a hundred years, as Pentagon intellectuals have predicted.

All wars in the past century began with the men who initiated them substituting their delusions, in which domestic political interests and personal ambitions often played a great part, for realistic evaluations of the titanic demands and consequences that modern warfare invariably imposes. They had neither the analytic clarity nor the honesty for such realism, and as careerists they often rejected pessimistic assessments of the risks that their intelligence organizations frequently produced. There were, obviously, many differences among these leaders, but with the possible exception of the Japanese in 1941, the men who led the major nations all shared a common consensus that they would emerge victorious from military conflicts. In a purely narrow technical sense, in the case of the Second World War, Roosevelt and Churchill were correct, and Nazism and Japanese imperialism were destroyed. But like those who so blithely entered the First World War, they refused to calculate the ultimate material and political costs that wars impose on themselves, their allies, or their enemies, and the spread of communism to Eastern Europe and a large part of Asia meant that politically the war was a disaster for them too. Military struggles have continuously turned out very differently than leaders imagined. They have been oblivious of surprises and have harbored false expectations; wars almost never conform to the convenient assumptions about how long conflicts will last and their decisive political consequences. The result was a twentieth century in which political upheavals were dominant: communism, fascism in various forms, and authoritarianism.

This persistent refusal to face reality's challenges and adjust foreign and military policies to them, to admit frankly that conventional wisdom and policies undermined the nation's security and long-term interests, has been virtually universal. Those who become the leaders of states are ultimately conformists on most crucial issues, and individuals who evaluate information in a rational manner—and therefore frequently criticize traditional premises—are weeded out early in their careers. The socialization process in most, even all nations eliminates such people, and ambitious ones comprehend full well the analytic and political boundaries upon which their future careers depend. Every large nation will have bureaucratic differences on implementing policies, but there is consensus on the policies themselves—a consensus that makes repeated errors increasingly likely. Leaders in every nation expect loyalty from potential decision makers, and except in rare cases, they get it. Political systems are not constructed to obtain and confront unpleasant facts, and they have few safeguards against irrational behavior. This myopia is increasingly dangerous.

The Roots of American Failure

Until the successful Soviet development of an atomic bomb in August 1949, the United States had complete confidence in its technology and its ability to maintain a relatively modest military budget of about $15 billion annually. The Truman administration believed, for good reason, that a war with the USSR was highly unlikely because Stalin's military and economic power was still feeble. But when the U.S. monopoly on the atomic bomb ended, the administration embarked on a far-reaching review of U.S. military power, and in April 1950 it decided to build a hydrogen bomb and to increase military spending to three to four times the fiscal 1949 outlay. What it could not predict was wars beginning in places that Moscow did not control. In 1949 the Communists took power in China, which was purely the consequence of the profound impact of Japan and the Second World War on that country. Stalin mistrusted Mao Tse-tung from the inception, and China was to prove—as Titoism had in Yugoslavia in 1948—that world communism was inherently a fissiparous, divided movement, united in little more than name. Washington over the next decade partially accepted this obvious reality, but it suited its propaganda for most of the 1950s to describe communism as entirely Moscow-controlled.

But while America's priorities strongly emphasized Europe, it also declared in January 1950 that Communist governments could not come to power in the remainder of Asia. This meant a much more active role in the Philippines, where a relatively small Communist insurgency was in progress. It also meant helping the French with arms and money to defeat the much more formidable Communist forces in Indochina—a decision whose ultimate consequences were far greater than American decision makers could imagine. When the North Korean army crossed the thirty-eighth parallel at the end of June 1950 the United States was already becoming involved in Asia even though it had no desire to sacrifice its Europe-first priorities and its emphasis on developing military power suited for warfare against modern concentrated military and urban targets. What it never acknowledged was that the outbreak of conflict anywhere in the world frequently imposed priorities upon it. In this fundamental sense, the United States has never been in full control of its foreign policy. But it has neither acknowledged nor admitted this fact.

America's leaders utterly failed to comprehend the Korean

War's potential military costs or its political and economic repercussions at home. From its inception it relied on air power and artillery—the intensive use of munitions. While much of the North's infrastructure was destroyed, the war ended in mid-1953 very close to the thirty-eighth parallel. The lavish use of firepower—three million tons, 43 percent of the tonnage the United States utilized in all of World War II—did not produce military victory. The North Koreans, joined by the Chinese at the end of 1950, adjusted their tactics to neutralize incredibly destructive and expensive technology and firepower. Roughly two million civilians died and half the southern population lost their homes or became refugees; killed and wounded soldiers on both sides were also about two million. The war ended in a stalemate, and the Republicans came to power in 1953 largely on a pledge to end the war.

The United States could easily get into wars, but its weaponry was all too fallible. Its military and political premises were gravely unrealistic. Its ally in the South, Syngman Rhee, was completely uncontrollable—at one point Washington even considered assassinating him. The credibility of its military power and technology was very much in doubt because it could not defeat enemies who decentralized their forces and utilized the weather and time to foil it; there was a cheap equivalent to its firepower. A war that the Americans intended to be short and limited lasted almost as long as World War II, only to end inconclusively. The United States still could not acknowledge the obvious reality, or the limits of high technology. It also depended on client regimes, which greatly complicated its efforts, and after its initial jingoism the American public tired of the war and proved inconstant, which in politics is fatal.

The Eisenhower administration and its successors were acutely aware of the potential inflationary impact of excessive military budgets, since inflation was one of the Korean War's many consequences. To a critical extent, its desire to restrain spending colored profoundly its definition of the challenges it confronted and the responses they demanded. Massive nuclear retaliation became the answer to Soviet power, but after the Korean experience it also realized that wars outside of Europe might absorb too large a proportion of American forces and that it needed a "flexible response" to Communist insurgencies and threats elsewhere. This took various forms. Military aid and training under the Eisenhower administration was quadrupled and the Southeast Asia Treaty Organization (SEATO) was created. In effect, the United States chose to respond to the Korean debacle by depending on proxies to do most of the fighting, tying its credibility to their destinies in ways whose implications it scarcely appreciated at the time. Under the Truman administration the CIA's clandestine services had expanded twenty times, to about six thousand people. Under Eisenhower another two thousand were added to it. The CIA became one of the decisive instruments of American foreign policy, especially in the Third World. Covert warfare was much less onerous, and Washington now had what it termed "plausible deniability" in its attempts to shape the future of hapless nations. Above all, it had flexibility and alternatives to using conventional force in confronting political developments of which it disapproved.[2]

Covert warfare and similar adaptations seemed to produce great successes, first in Iran in 1953 and in Guatemala in 1954, and then in numerous other places. It seemed to be an uncomplicated and inexpensive way for the United States to replace regimes and control the destinies of nations. After 1955 the United States also began to intimidate those it disapproved of by "showing the flag" much more frequently, sending its boats and manpower to various nations to make certain that local political and military instability did not produce outcomes Washington deemed dangerous. There were 215 such instances of "force without war" during 1946–75. Some were minor, but others were major and potentially dangerous, and the United States exhibited its power virtually everywhere.[3] Lebanon in 1958, the Dominican Republic in 1961–66, Jordan in 1970, and yet other examples I deal with later: these victories restored the confidence that America's leaders had lost after the Korean stalemate. By and large, such interventions guaranteed that the Third World's political evolution would not clash with U.S. interests, tipping the balance not merely away from communism but in favor of conservative and often reactionary regimes both unable and unwilling to meet their peoples' material and political needs. A large number of them violated their citizens' human rights, ranging from torture and imprisonment to press censorship, and many were recipients of U.S. arms and police and military training missions, which became ubiquitous after the early 1950s. To a critical extent, successive Washington administrations made state-sponsored terrorism possible.

The United States after 1947 attempted to guide and control a very large part of the change that occurred throughout the world, and a significant part of what is wrong with it today is the result of America's interventions. Others have paid for their consequences, and now the United States too must pay.

The Korean War also intensified the United States' dependence on imports of raw materials, primarily from the Third

World. All its leaders were conscious of the importance of these imports, an awareness that constantly influenced foreign policy decisions. Only 5 percent of its total consumption of metals, excluding gold and iron, was imported in the 1920s, but 38 percent was imported from 1940–49, and 48 percent in the following decade. America's growth was linked to access to absolutely essential imports, the Western Hemisphere being its single largest supplier of vital metals, but the Middle East was crucial for petroleum.

What began as part of an effort to make its military responses both cheaper and more flexible, to resolve the limits and contradictions of its strategic doctrines, also made it possible for the United States to involve itself in many more potentially dangerous situations. It thereby became far more dependent on the wisdom and fate of its proxies, such as Ngo Dinh Diem in South Vietnam after 1954 and the shah in Iran from 1953 to 1979. But the dictators' soldiers and guns could not stabilize the politics of these and innumerable other places. What were intended to be small decisions in fact often became incremental errors that pushed Washington in unanticipated and unintended directions, and they were eventually to prove decisive to America's preoccupations and interests—in Southeast Asia and ultimately also in the Middle East. The result was that the United States lost more control over its military and foreign policy. There were many successes for it, some of which we know little about because they were covert; but the failures eventually led it to escalate its involvement in various nations to avert the appearance of impotence.

Today we live under the shadow of these failures.

The Vietnam War and America's Strategic Dilemma[4]

Vietnam was to become the ultimate example of how infinitely complex social realities in the Third World had become, and of the danger to the United States in its fatal dependence on venal rulers. It exposed the fragility of the foundations on which American foreign policy was based. Initially Washington responded to the events in Vietnam in the larger context of its ongoing search for a decisive strategy relevant for the entire Third World. The efficacy of limited war, its new weapons technology, its credibility, the domino theory, political rivalries and ambitions, and much else became tangled in a skein of interrelated causes. It was virtually preordained that the United States would somewhere attempt to confirm its credibility after the crucial failures it had suffered in Korea, Cuba, and elsewhere. Vietnam was to become the epitome of the postwar crisis in American power and ambition, a testimony to its inability to articulate a successful military and political basis for establishing a global socioeconomic environment congenial to its interests and desires.

The causal elements of the crisis that existed in Vietnam existed in many other countries, and still do. There was a grossly inequitable land distribution, and a corrupt leader whom the United States selected and who ruled with an iron hand. After nine years with Diem the CIA aided in his assassination, but there was no alternative to repeated American military escalation, and in the end approximately two million U.S. military personnel served there. The cycle of corruption and instability, the massive use of fifteen million tons of munitions, and the conflict's intensity and length, produced the longest war and the most important defeat in American history. High mobility and firepower, the latest military concepts, virtually unlimited expenses—all were in vain. There were approximately one million deaths, at least half of the people were driven from their homes, and far more military aid—sophisticated aviation and equipment—was given to its proxies than they knew how to utilize. By 1968 the CIA and other official experts warned policy makers in Washington that the war was going badly and victory might elude them. The American public grew weary and critical of the war, Congress eventually responded to this mood, and the soldiers they sent were demoralized to an extent that had no precedent. In April 1975 the war ended in a total, ignominious disaster for the United States, largely because it had depended on politically shrewd but venal, corrupt proxies.

The crisis in America's foreign and military strategy that the Vietnam War created was matched by the grave divisions in the Communist world and the ultimate demise of most of these regimes. But while the fall of communism gave a momentary breathing spell to the United States, in the end it ushered in a far more complex and unstable world, the grave consequences of which we are now experiencing. The CIA had repeatedly argued that the Soviet leaders feared an American nuclear attack (many British leaders also thought a preemptive American strike a very real possibility), and that while they were developing a modern arsenal only as a deterrent, the Soviet leaders believed that they would prevail by nonmilitary means or not at all. As Marxists they were certain that the ineluctable march of history was on their side. But their power over China—which America's leaders for well over a decade argued publicly was absolute—was far more nominal than real, and by the early

1960s they were deadly enemies. In Eastern Europe the Soviet influence withered away more gradually, save for the open break with Yugoslavia in 1948. The USSR simply could not afford to both build a modern army and shower economic and military aid abroad. Moscow wasted immense sums in nations where it had very little, if any, political influence. And while Soviet power was disintegrating, significant parts of the Third World were being economically and demographically traumatized. The single most important cause for this shock was that export-oriented, capital-intensive agriculture drove peasants off the land and into cities. The political reaction to it took many forms, but, especially in Central America, they were leftist only in the broad sense of that term.

In brief, large parts of the Third World were being destabilized economically even as communism was disintegrating and eventually disappearing as a historical force. The United States chose to respond to the inevitable social and political consequences of such objective trends as growing challenges, but it also intervened actively elsewhere for a variety of reasons certain to win it enemies. It supported Pakistan in its confrontation with India over the Bangladesh secession only because it was an old ally employing American weapons; in fact, American leaders also believed the secessionists had good reasons for wanting independence. Nixon supported Ferdinand Marcos's declaration of martial law in the Philippines in the fall of 1972. In Angola in 1975 Kissinger ignored the advice of his advisers, and the CIA supported movements about which it knew very little because he felt that after the Vietnam humiliation it was more essential than ever to show that the United States still had power—its "credibility" required action for its own sake. To this day Angola remains war-torn. The deaths and injuries since the conflict began run well over a hundred thousand, and over one-third of the population has been displaced at some time and become refugees. There were innumerable other instances where the United States sought only to confirm the credibility of its power, intervening everywhere but especially giving its support and loyalty to Third World tyrants and corruptionists who acted as faithful proxies. This fixation—and blindness in estimating the long-term consequences of its actions—grew as Soviet power, which had inhibited America in some places, was weakening gravely.

The Structural Causes of Third World Crises

Poverty is one of the crucial root causes of every form of political instability, from religious fundamentalism to revolutionary movements, that pose challenges to the United States' goal of reorganizing the world to suit its own definitions—and interests. This was true a century ago, and it is just as valid today. The United States has been amazingly successful, working through the International Monetary Fund (IMF), the World Bank, and its own corporations as well as those in Europe and Japan who share America's desire to see the world "globalized," in opening key countries to private investors and businesses, and in restructuring the world in what it alleges is its own image. The entire former Soviet bloc, China, and Vietnam have also accepted the "Washington consensus" and are attempting to impose the "globalization" model on their now capitalist economies. This very broad and essentially vague consensus—which attributes a mystical efficiency and rationality to the market and competition—among those who guide the economic affairs of nations is both astonishing and virtually universal. But it also ignores history entirely, for the United States has always behaved very differently, defending its farmers, steel producers, and countless other business constituencies with subsidies, antidumping quotas, and the like. The gap between the theory of "globalization" and the actual practice of the states that urge others to implement it is enormous. To the United States it means free mobility of every form of capital, but to Japan and East Asia it means unfettered exports—and every nation, including America, implements it to suit its own interests and exceptions.

But the dilemma facing the Americans and all those who share their faith is that poverty—and the instability that it aggravates—have remained in the midst of prosperity for some. The failure to eliminate or even significantly reduce poverty leaves them with a structural legacy in which desperation thrives. Sooner or later they will have to pay the unknown but frequently substantial political and social price that structural inequities such as these create. The wars in Afghanistan for the past quarter century have a variety of sources, but poverty and the conditions it produces—above all illiteracy and the religious and ethnic fanaticism that it nourishes—have certainly been important.

Statistics on poverty are only rough estimates and keep changing, but poverty has untold human—and often political—consequences, and it has persisted. Even before much of the full impact of the 1997 East Asia turmoil could be felt elsewhere, the number of people in the Third World (excluding China) living below the World Bank's meager poverty standard of $1.79

per day (in 1993 purchasing power) had increased 15 percent from 1987 to 1998—to 1.4 billion people. Eastern and central Europe, Latin America, and sub-Saharan Africa—regions where the IMF was most influential—experienced a higher incidence of poverty from 1980 to 1997, while poverty declined in booming East and South Asia, the Middle East, and North Africa. But the financial crisis in East Asia that began in the summer of 1997 caused the real 1998 per capita household income to decline 20 percent in South Korea, 12 percent in the Philippines, and 24 percent in Indonesia. And by late 1999 the crisis had pushed from 15 million to 75 million people below the poverty line. Most lived in Asia, whose integration in the "globalized" world economy was trumpeted as the source of their prosperity. They have now been subjected to globalization's many inherent instabilities.

Increasingly unequal income distribution in much of the Third World explains part of this persistence, and grossly inadequate economic growth explains much of the remainder. In Russia and Eastern Europe this inequality, stagnant and declining economies, and the abolition of virtually all forms of social protection have added greatly to the world's poverty and human and social problems. IMF insistence on balancing budgets has caused many poor countries to reduce the proportion of their gross domestic product allocated to health and education. But education, health, and transfer programs in developing nations did not reverse growing income inequality, and in many nations they benefited mainly upper-income groups. Latin America fared especially badly, with utterly inadequate social safety nets, and in some nations there was a reversal during the 1990s of gains made in preceding decades. Argentina, which took the IMF's guidance on virtually all economic matters and accumulated enormous debts, is the best-known example of nations now in serious decline. But in fact it is quite typical of the way many nations have managed their economic policies.[5]

Such nuances in economic, social, and political transformations have made instability and great changes inherent in the modern historical experience. This chronic disorder, in turn, has left the United States floundering for an effective strategic synthesis. The self-confident optimism that characterized its efforts after the mid-1950s is now largely gone. Counterinsurgency and a reliance on massive firepower failed in Vietnam, and while the Pentagon has had plenty of theorists who could concoct assorted doctrines, in fact America's policies since then have been ad hoc and incremental, ranging from barely concealed covert aid of arms and advisers to the contras in Nicaragua and the mujahideen in Afghanistan during the 1980s, to the outright use of American troops in Grenada in 1983, to the Iranian hostage rescue debacle in April 1980. Both in theory and financially, the Reagan administration after 1981 favored a massive arms buildup. Doctrinally, in November 1984 it articulated the "Weinberger Doctrine" to warn that it would utilize its military power massively should it fight again. The threat was sufficiently vague to frighten the Russians with visions of America using its nuclear weapons in a first strike, but it also caused many in the CIA and Washington to share the Russians' deep anxieties.

In practice, however, America's responses to military challenges have never been consistent or coherent, and the Weinberger Doctrine became just one of many ideas that Washington has concocted—and usually forgotten. The United States has persisted in its futile search for a doctrinally logical justification for employing its massive military power, but even the domino theory remained conventional wisdom on how political change occurred in the Third World. Above all, whether Republicans or Democrats, America's leaders failed to comprehend the negative long-term political, economic, and ideological consequences of its policies in much of the world. This was their calamitous oversight, because the world is far more complicated than weaponry can cope with. Countless U.S. interventions have done great harm while solving few problems; they have been counterproductive by every criterion.

The United States has almost always succeeded in its military efforts, whether covert or open. It has won, at least in the short run, most of its interventions. In Cuba it failed because its proxies were venal and its efforts were incompetent. There was, in many regards, a basis for its overweening self-confidence, but these victories failed to take into account the long-term political and ideological consequences of what seemed to be successes. Moreover, America's losses in Vietnam and Korea were crucial because they revealed how finite was its military power when it confronted able enemies ready to make the most of the terrain and space, enemies able to neutralize its firepower and concentrated forces. Few, if any, in Washington seriously analyzed these defeats. But they have eventually proved to be decisive, and they are today more crucial than nominal military victories.

The breakup of the Soviet Union only intensified the official U.S. confusion, since no one could any longer explain why problems arise by referring to some nefarious forces in Moscow. Indeed, as the Soviets no longer played their inhibiting and essentially conservative role, the world became less safe and more unstable than ever. Even worse, the Pentagon's strategy and military equipment were heavily oriented to Soviet targets and Eastern European conditions, and now these were irrelevant. An obvious and visible enemy had been very useful for Washington's leaders after 1946, if only because they could often convince an occasionally reticent Congress and American public that more arms spending was justified. Communist parties no longer existed but change still occurred, indeed more rapidly than ever, and political groups of all other ideological persuasions were just as active. Washington refused to acknowledge the role that the Soviets played after 1947 in discouraging radicalism throughout the world, and that the Western European parties most under their control were often docile members of ruling political coalitions. In China, especially, they urged the Communists to pursue a much more moderate line, laying the basis for the subsequent break with Mao Tse-tung. But today the original justification for the United States' virtually hegemonic global leadership pretensions—with its bases and massive military hardware almost everywhere—is now gone.

The dissolution of the Soviet Union has left the United States feeling stronger than ever, but in reality it is also more vulnerable, and it has only increased the risks it is now taking with the welfare and security of its own people.

5

STRATEGIC CONFUSIONS

The United States has never fought the wars it expected to fight, and its grand military strategy has compounded wishful thinking and—as Vietnam proved—its unintended step-by-step escalation in the face of equally unanticipated challenges. Strategy has also been, in large part, the product of the three major Pentagon services advocating competitive approaches which justify their obtaining as large a share of the military budget as possible. This has meant a much greater emphasis on highly sophisticated weaponry and, above all, on air power capable of delivering nuclear weapons. In part, the United States has also prepared to fight its next war as if it might be very much like the last one. For fifty years it armed itself to fight the USSR by threatening its destruction with nuclear weapons and by sending its ultramodern military forces across Eastern Europe's relatively congenial terrain, notwithstanding the CIA's consistent opinion—which was ignored—that such a conflict would probably not be necessary. But now the Soviet Union no longer exists and Eastern Europe is composed of friendly nations, and America's other real and potential adversaries have few, if any, concentrated, urbanized targets against which to concentrate its vast armada of missiles and planes.

What America does best is spend money as if weapons provide solutions to political and social problems. They do not. Arms can destroy people, including its enemies, but they at best only temporarily defer the core reasons why most crises occur in various nations in the first place—reasons that are overwhelmingly political and economic. This is one of the crucial reasons why the United States lost the war in Vietnam. The other is that its technology and its basic strategy are unsuited to the physical and economic realities of much of the Third World, where it fought all its wars from 1945 to 1999. This is why it made war for nearly four years in Korea only to end in a stalemate. Even in strictly military terms, the United States has not won unconditional victories in its three major wars since 1945 in which its own troops were involved for a sustained period, and it did not win its two protracted land wars—Korea and Vietnam. In the Gulf War against Iraq—which lasted only forty-seven days—it easily drove the Iraqi forces out of Kuwait, but Saddam Hussein is still in power, and the Gulf area is more politically destabilized than ever; and as I argue in the second chapter, even this war would never have occurred had the United States not grossly interfered in the region's affairs from 1953 onward. It can mount spectacular forays against weak nations, and some are successful, like those against the tiny states of Grenada in October 1983 or Panama in December 1989; but others—such as its failed rescue of hostages in Iran in April 1980 or its commando raid against Mogadishu, Somalia, in September 1993 (eighteen Americans were killed and scores were wounded)—have been equally spectacular failures.

America's leaders have ignored whatever lessons their lost wars should have taught them, for defeat is not an option for them. The United States has been alone in its readiness since 1947 to intervene with its own overt or covert military power virtually anywhere in the world, and repeated political or military failures have not discouraged it. Whenever their own intelligence, as in Vietnam, warned them that they were not succeeding and might very well end in failure, they have ignored it. Even good news, like the grave weaknesses which led to the collapse of the Soviet Union, was ignored because it undermined the political agendas of various administrations and their appeals for greater military spending. Most of the recent major crises the United States has confronted, even some senior Pentagon officials now confess, were unforeseen. But their answer to this dilemma is "to build capabilities for the future which aren't oriented toward a specific conflict or a specific war plan," as if the same weapons fit all possible challenges, which they have not in the past and will not in the future. "[T]he whole last century is littered with failures of prediction," Paul Wolfowitz presciently observed in June 2001; then he immediately proceeded to ignore his own words.[1] And, of course, after the disastrous failure to predict the September 11 calamity, the Bush administration wants to better coordinate and upgrade the thirteen agencies in the intelligence business.

The men who have run the United States and the Pentagon are confused, and even some of its own senior officers have openly detailed its various malaises. We can ignore the fact that after the National Security Act of 1947 much of the time of the four services was spent undercutting one another and fighting for a larger share of the military budget, which was overgenerous by any criterion. There was still a much larger consensus that bound them together, although they were often loath to admit it, and their common fixation on Soviet power was the main core of their irrelevance. Explaining why it lost the Vietnam War remained exceedingly troublesome for the United States, and it responded to this catastrophe by concocting new weapons and doctrines—in effect ignoring past failures and relying on what is politically the national disease, congenital optimism, and, of course, expensive procurements. Failure is not in the politicians' or military's vocabulary, and this leads to yet more adventures—some successful and others not. It is also the principal reason why war has reached the American homeland.

America's goals in the world have not changed since the end of the Second World War, and communism's collapse has led to a greater emphasis on economic rather than strategic objectives. The "uninhibited access to key markets, energy supplies, and strategic resources," to cite the Pentagon's 1996 annual defense report, was crucial, even if that report could not identify who could resist the United States' "unilateral use of military power" to protect its "vital national interests." There are also mystical elements in the United States' vaguely defined mission to reform the way the world has existed and operated, but at its core these always identify the world's interests and America's as one and the same—and its unlimited hubris is essentially self-serving. But enlarging the number of "free-market" nations, too, was no longer a problem; both China and Vietnam also believe passionately in the market and are well on their way to becoming capitalist in all but name. It thought an "unpredictable" and "uncertain future" was likely, and that the world "remains a complex, dynamic, and dangerous place," but it could not pin down the reasons now that communism had virtually ceased to exist. It referred to "failed states" and "dangerous technologies" that were proliferating, but it was painfully silent on where and how all this was occurring. What was plainly clear was that the American military wanted to justify the budget that would allow it to modernize, "to retain military superiority."[2] But if nuclear power is the criterion, it has it already and no longer needs to spend prodigiously.

What was gone, as one general told a Senate committee in January 1998, was "the bi-polar nature of superpower competition [that] allowed for substantial continuity in U.S. defense planning and force development."[3] Variations of these themes suffuse all Pentagon justifications for higher budgets. For the five years ending in fiscal 2005 the Pentagon asked for $1.6 trillion! It wanted more modern weapons—nuclear, conventional, anything—against unnamed enemies and targets. In reality, there are no longer credible enemies, but no American administration will admit what is obvious.

The United States seeks a decisive preeminence in any future war against a modern enemy, and above all control of the skies—which includes all forms of communications. In principle, it has staked out its ultimate responsibility for whatever political and economic goals it deems congenial to its values and interests in every part of the world. It wishes to be able to do everything involving force, whether quite minor or very vast. In practice, it expects the Europeans to play a substantially greater role in keeping the peace in that region, and it hopes that military aid and training will suffice elsewhere—as in Colombia. Avoiding overcommitting American manpower is still a practical and political necessity, and the Pentagon is extremely sensitive to how the Vietnam War became highly unpopular among the American public. It does not exclude ground warfare, which has a potentially very great political price because it has no guarantee of quick military success against able enemies—and time is the one thing the Pentagon cannot expect to have in unlimited quantities. But its statements in the *Quadrennial Defense Review Report* of September 2001 and earlier make it perfectly clear that it wishes military supremacy in every corner of the globe. "America's security role in the world is unique. . . . The United States has interests, responsibilities, and commitments that span the world."[4] But attaining it is quite another matter.

The Clinton administration encouraged the Pentagon's insatiable demands. In January 2000—with an eye on the November 2000 presidential election—it added $115 billion to the Pentagon's five-year Future Years Defense Plan, extending to 2005, far more than what the Republicans were calling for. It refused to sign the Ottawa Landmines Treaty, it opposed many of the terms of a proposed treaty controlling the small-arms trade that the National Rifle Association disliked, and it strongly opposed linking burgeoning American arms exports to criteria on human rights and democracy. The United States' already leading share of the world arms market grew even larger: from 32 percent of the world trade in weapons in 1987 to 43 percent by 1997. Of the 140 nations it gave or sold arms to in 1995, 90 percent were not democracies or abused human rights. Not counting the ballistic missile defense system, at the beginning of 2001 the Pentagon had over a half trillion dollars in major weapons systems in the pipeline, all of which the Clinton administration had approved. It accounted in 1995 for nearly two-thirds of the world's spending on military research and development and its share of global military spending increased from 31 percent in 1985 to 36 percent in fiscal 2000—and today it is even higher. Along with its close allies, it accounts for about two-thirds of all military spending. In reality, there was no foreign military threat to even remotely justify these expenditures, only politically powerful contractors who would disappear if the Pentagon did not buy their wares.

The war in Kosovo that began on March 24, 1999, profoundly reoriented the Pentagon, if only because NATO's form of coalition warfare proved time-consuming and cumbersome, and produced endless frustrations. The fractious European nations argued with one another and with the Americans, and ultimately they refused to pay for their pretensions. But militarily, although it took far longer than the United States had predicted and the Serbs fought for seventy-eight days, the war nominally ended triumphantly. Yet, although more than a thousand planes were involved, the goal of preventing the expulsion of Kosovo's ethnic Albanians was not attained; rather, the expulsion accelerated. Politically, however, although his fellow Serbs drove Milosevic from power and he ended up in The Hague on charges of being a war criminal, the region is more destabilized than ever. As predicted by many, Albanian irredentism, which is largely Muslim, spread to Macedonia, where a sporadic civil war has begun. Indeed, a goodly number of those the United States aided as "freedom fighters" were also involved in criminal activities or were Islamic fanatics with ties to Iran or bin Laden.

By the time the Clinton administration left office even establishment critics believed its military and diplomatic priorities were profoundly awry and contradictory. A few former top officers said as much publicly. There simply was no inhibition on America's ambitions even though it had shown time and again that it was physically unable to do everything it was committed to accomplishing, and repeated political failures only confirmed that the world had problems about which the United States could do nothing and it was to everyone's interest that it avoid getting involved in them altogether. In reality, its priorities were often determined where there was shooting or wherever the American government had the desire to intervene, a fetish that its uninhibited foreign and military doctrines and goals made inevitable. The Pentagon's new emphasis on a "capability-based" strategy admits that past priorities and perceived specific threats were essentially wrong, and that the basic assumptions that guided U.S. grand strategy since 1946 were erroneous. Neither its resources, its interests, nor political sagacity warranted its unlimited pretensions, which only lead to more failures. That is where it is at today.

Apart from much of the world developing a growing dislike or hatred of the United States, its self-appointed global mission created a hothouse for irresponsible and increasingly dangerous Americans in power. This has been the case for well over a half century, when the British government feared in 1950 that the United States would embark on a preventive nuclear war against the Soviet Union. In the late summer of 1961 the Kennedy administration considered a range of nuclear first strikes against the USSR, and it even drew up the necessary plans. When Rumsfeld became secretary of defense the new president agreed with him that the nation's credibility would be weakened unless military power was utilized whenever there was any threat to American interests and it showed it was not averse to taking risks. An even more aggressive foreign policy was preordained. Since September 11, 2001, the Pentagon has harbored a group of civilian hawks, led by Undersecretary Paul Wolfowitz, who in turn have marshaled conservative intellectual strategists who advocate extending the war to Iraq and have even set their sights on Somalia, Syria, Iran, and elsewhere. Their ranks at times include Defense Secretary Donald H. Rumsfeld and Vice President Dick Cheney; their opponents, Secretary of State Colin Powell, most generals, and the CIA. Ultimately, the president will decide. But there have been many such extremists among policy makers since the cold war began. That communism disappeared without revolution or war makes no difference to their paranoid interpretations of world affairs.

Wanted: Credible Enemies

Although NATO emerged more united than divided on the war in Kosovo, whatever goodwill remained among its members was largely dissipated by the antimissile shield Washington advocated to protect the American continent from an attack by technically sophisticated adversaries. Such a shield has been on the drawing boards for decades. Successive administrations have mentioned North Korea, Iran, and Iraq as the possible culprits—the president at the beginning of 2002 designated them as an "axis of evil"—but no nation possesses the technical capacity to inflict sufficient damage before it is utterly devastated by an American riposte. Indeed, Iraq probably has no effective missiles whatsoever. An arms race exists in South Asia and the Middle East, but it is between regional enemies and is scarcely a threat to the United States, with its overwhelming nuclear supremacy. In fact, however, the Pentagon implied the real enemy was China and perhaps others, although stating this openly would be impolitic. Moreover, should the ABM work, then mutual deterrence, the basis of the United States' strategic nuclear theory for decades, would end; it could strike any nation with impunity first, whether using conventional or nuclear weapons, and destroy any riposte. The only credible nuclear power would be the nation with an ABM—the United States. It would make its military adventures much more feasible, and therefore all the more likely.

The prospect of America building the ABM had by early 2000 created deep dissension within the NATO alliance, alienated Russia (its 1972 treaty on missiles with the United States would have to be annulled), and spread suspicion in every direction. But such a system became a football in American politics and a very large plum for defense contractors. It was all liabilities, and while its research had cost at least $71 billion as of 1999, it was technically and politically a very bad idea—save among some contractors.

First, the United States' allies thought the idea dangerous, and so did the Russians. Rand experts concluded that it would be "practical and economical" for Russia to overcome the American system, but nominally Russia was no longer an enemy.[5] But the Congressional Budget Office in April 2000 wrote that even a limited system would cost $60 billion—and might not work. At the beginning of 2002 it estimated that an operational system would cost about a quarter-trillion dollars by 2025. Indeed, the system was potentially open-ended in terms of expenses, and every phase of it had to be technically perfect. At worst, Rand experts warned, a partial system would offer no protection, and prove a great waste of money. That is exactly what has happened.

It is astonishing that the ABM has been taken seriously, since it was first proposed by Ronald Reagan in 1983 and has yet to be proven feasible. But its persistence until this day reflects the initial fascination that the Pentagon has for supersophisticated technology and the extent to which it can be impervious to the obvious political implication of its fads. And, of course, there have been immense sums waiting for defense contractors able to get pieces of the action. These contractors, especially Lockheed Martin and Boeing, were crucial in eventually reversing the CIA's technical assessment in the mid-1990s that Iran, North Korea, and other "rogue states" were incapable of building a credible missile delivery system in the foreseeable future. Technically, the ABM system the Clinton administration proposed could not distinguish between real warheads and decoys, and its advocates were accused of rigging its tests. By 2000 there were also increasingly strong opponents of the ABM within the Pentagon, who thought it a waste of funds better spent in other ways. By late 2000 most of the Joint Chiefs of Staff were among them.

American-Russian relations were also increasingly muddied by this issue. President Putin proposed new European defense arrangements. He also went to North Korea in July 2000 in the hope of getting sufficient verbal assurances from Kim Jong II to stop Washington from pursuing what appeared like an ABM system which in fact, if not in intent, was aimed at Russia. America's friends in Europe saw it as an example of its emerging unilateralism. Even Defense Secretary William S. Cohen, the ABM's strongest advocate within the administration, confessed that he was uncertain of the vast, expensive enterprise's technological premises: "That remains to be determined." An "act of terrorism taking place on the United States is more likely than [an] intercontinental ballistic missile," he conceded, and all the American intelligence agencies at the beginning of 2002 concurred that weapons of mass destruction are more likely to be delivered by some means—boats, airplanes, and the like—against which the ABM is utterly useless.[6] The Pentagon tested the system in early July 2000, and it failed again. By then the administration had alienated its allies in Europe, embittered relations with Russia, and caused China to worry that it was really the ABM's principal target. In fact, the Clinton administration also wanted to help Vice President Al Gore get elected, and so it favored the ABM to make it appear as if the Democrats were as strong on defense as their opponents.

But George Bush became president. And while he too strongly favored the ABM during the election, he left it to his new defense secretary to quell growing dissent within the Pentagon and Congress.

What the American government lacked after the demise of the USSR was a credible enemy, one that could unite Congress and the public. A sense of danger and fear was essential to the American effort to maintain its hegemony over its allies and to justify immense military funding from a Congress unwilling to casually accept deficit financing and higher taxes. Without such an enemy, the United States had to find much more convincing justifications for its policies and actions, and not only was it loath to do so, it could not. This obligated the Pentagon and the government to define a strategy which justified maintaining its bases and manpower overseas and spending huge sums. Although they surely outlined plans for a "robust" presence elsewhere, East Asia by the end of the last decade was deemed the place where the United States would be most involved over the next decade. About one hundred thousand men would remain stationed in the region to implement a policy of "robust engagement."

Against whom? This has not been answered, for an obvious reason: no nation in the region will risk confronting the United States, because it has nuclear weapons and has declared its readiness to use them. The tension in Korea was on the way to a solution, if only because the North Korean economy was a disaster and it was merely a question of time before the South—either de facto or even formally—took over what is an endemic basket-case economy. In 1999 North Korea was being portrayed as perhaps the leading "rogue" state, but by mid-2000 it had agreed to cease testing missiles, which eliminated the main justification for the ABM project. Only China has the capacity and, allegedly, the will to become the United States' unnamed "peer competitor." It has nuclear weapons and missiles, and while the Pentagon talked of building confidence with it, "the gap that exists in [China's] strategic visions" could lead to "military accidents and miscalculations." [7]

The one problem, as the Pentagon's own experts told it, was that China was by the end of the decade eager to embrace "multilateralism" and had effectively given up socialism in all but name. Objectively, China is a capitalist economy, abandoning quickly the state economic sector, and the Communist Party's decision in mid-2001 to allow businessmen to join transformed it into a much broader instrument of the economic as well as political ruling class. China had in fact helped the

Americans during the 1980s to finance and arm the Afghan mujahideen to fight the Soviets. And although the bombing of the Chinese embassy in Belgrade in May 1999 and the accidental crash of American and Chinese planes over Hainan Island while the former was on an intelligence mission in April 2001 brought out a great deal of latent Chinese anti-Americanism and nationalism, its rulers are experts in stifling dissent. China's rulers want to do business, and their highest priorities, by far, are economic; their adhesion to the World Trade Organization is the surest indication that they seek to be integrated into a capitalist world economy. China was encouraged to develop "a stake in the system" and did so; axiomatically, it became far stronger industrially in the process. China is well on its way to becoming a great economic power. There is still a Chinese military establishment, and like many nations—above all, the United States—it sells weapons wherever there is a market. And though China still claims Taiwan is a province, the Taiwanese have invested heavily in China, so this very old dispute is hardly a cause for serious worry.

But at the beginning of 2001 and until September 11 China was the United States' potential threat of choice, and the justification for its extravagant spending policies. China was opposed to the ABM, but so were many of the United States' oldest allies. "We are competitors," Secretary Rumsfeld observed in January. "They are seeking influence in the region, and we are in the region. We see their defense budget increasing by double digits every year." [8] Rumsfeld was charged with the enormously complex task of reorienting the Pentagon, both to make it more efficient and to prepare it for the most likely political and military challenges. This survey and plan for reform, which was eventually to be presented in the *Quadrennial Defense Review Report* at the end of September 2001, from its inception appeared likely to stress the Chinese threat. Rumsfeld's key adviser, Andrew Marshall, the head of the Pentagon's internal think tank in charge of the review, was known to have long advocated emphasizing the alleged China menace. He favored shifting much of the military's assets from Europe, where American vital interests were no longer challenged, to Asia. "What do I think about China?" Rumsfeld stated in July of that year. "My view of China is that it's future is not written, and it is being written." Its succession process was unpredictable, the military might jockey civilians out of power—China was unstable, "an authoritarian system, a communist dictatorship," but also increasingly powerful. In a statement certain to make its leaders fear the new administration, at the end of August Wolfowitz declared, "[O]ver the long run the Chinese political system is going to have to change."[9] The United States simply did not trust China, which in turn sought to make defensive accords with Russia and the former Soviet Central Asian republics, who were supposed to ignore that most of its nuclear missiles could reach only Russian and Asian targets.

Making China the principal (but surely not exclusive) nemesis was only part of the pending review. The Pentagon had suffered from strategic confusion for years and had failed in its two longest wars, Korea and Vietnam. Weapons and firepower still hypnotized it, but it had lost some of its confidence that merely possessing them led automatically to victory. It should have been much more critical of its well-worn and older premises than it was, but Rumsfeld and his colleagues were somewhat readier than their predecessors to examine the military's functions. Leaks on their contemplated report abounded in the press. Rumsfeld especially wanted to change the way that military branches were organized to make them ostensibly more functional; but the services fought all changes, especially those that reduced the size of their forces, equipment, and budgets.

All efforts since 1947 to reform the services since their basic organization was created have floundered because of intense service resistance. While many have attempted to rationalize the military establishment, no defense secretary has more than nibbled at their expensive vested interests. There are 225 military bases in the United States, many of them plums to friendly congressmen, and they could not be closed with impunity, for they too were costly vested interests from past strategies, all of which were increasingly irrelevant. Thirty-three B-1 bombers, intended to penetrate Soviet airspace, were no longer needed, but their two bases could not be touched; they were in Texas and the home state of the Senate majority leader. About a quarter of the existing "infrastructure" is superfluous. By the end of 2001 the administration had gotten Congress to agree to close a few bases by 2005. This was two years later than the Pentagon wished and also allowed congressmen ample time to save them. And many expensive and largely superfluous weapons were still slated for purchase because the producers had friends in Congress. Rumsfeld wanted more missile defenses, ultramodern equipment, and flexibility in how to utilize the military services—and he met ferocious resistance. It was essential to save money through internal changes as well as to obtain more from Congress. "This is by far the most disorganized effort I've ever seen," one general told a reporter. In strategic terms, the military now planned to win one rather than two major wars, for Kosovo had shown that an obdurate, well-entrenched enemy was a much greater challenge and might take far longer than expected to defeat. More important, the Pentagon's specific conflict and war plan was now, as Wolfowitz put it, "somewhat hazier." [10] At the end of June Rumsfeld admitted that the forthcoming review would only partially alter the Pentagon's expensive, entrenched bad habits; at least another year would be required before his reforms were completed. In fact, he had run up against the same military resistance that has for decades defeated all efforts to make the Pentagon operate more efficiently and economically. In the end, after bitter brawls, the officers succeeded—and Rumsfeld failed.

September 11 changed everything, and those writing the highly touted review were told to forget their many months of labor and to start again, to "think outside the box." In reality, the September 11 events gave them an excuse to avoid the embarrassing compromises and discontent they had appeared destined to produce. China instantly ceased to be America's most likely enemy although the Bush administration still regards its drive to become a great power in the region and its progress in developing mobile strategic missiles as very dangerous. Indeed, when the *Quadrennial Report* was issued at the end of that month, as scheduled, allusions to China were buried in rhetoric. "Maintaining a stable balance in Asia will be a complex task. The possibility exists that a military competitor with a formidable resource base will emerge in the region" was as close as it came to mentioning it. [11] That problem, at least, had temporarily disappeared. But if China was really a threat to the United States before September 11, then it was still one after that date, unless the very proposition was highly irresponsible, dangerous Pentagon rhetoric to justify its budget requests. China's military budget is about one-eighth of the Pentagon's, and it has about 150 strategic nuclear weapons—compared with over 6,000 in America's arsenal. In fact, China's nuclear posture is a minimum deterrent only—at the beginning of 2002 it had a maximum of thirty ICBMs. While the number will increase over the coming years, there was no reason to assume that the Chinese would be any more likely than the Soviets to take adventurist risks.

September 11 saved the Pentagon from great embarrassment and the need to admit that it was confused and divided and that the military services would resist major changes. The document was completely rewritten in a few weeks to respond to an entirely new situation the military establishment had scarcely contemplated. Congress subsequently appeared ready to approve almost whatever budget increases the calamity seemed to warrant, and there was no longer a concern with waste or deficits. Rumsfeld immediately shifted his statements from getting the maximum from a finite budget to appeals for much more funding, adding that it is beneficial to all nations. "We are perfectly capable of spending whatever we need to spend. The world economy depends on the United States [contributing] to peace and stability. That is what underpins the economic health of the world, including the United States." [12]

Yesterday's budget-balancing conservatives became deficit spenders. The size of the military was left untouched, but— money notwithstanding—the basic strategic problems the United States has inherited over a half century still remain. Indeed, they are far greater than ever. Is it possible for it to operate effectively in all places? Are its goals clarified? Do its priorities and national interest really match its virtually unlimited but vague military commitments?

The United States would now develop a "capability-based strategy" because in the "much more complex" world that now existed all that seemed possible was to anticipate "the kinds of capabilities that could threaten us much better than we can predict exactly where that threat will come from or what entity or what country." The report itself was sufficiently ambiguous enough in its prescriptions to gloss over rivalries between the different services. Otherwise it was familiar. It desired improved intelligence but admitted that the future adversary, its location, or even its very form was now an open question. Forward stationing, airlift, sealift, research and development of new technology, and the like were essential to deny "asymmetric advantages to adversaries," but the report repeatedly stressed that the Pentagon could no longer predict the identities of the actors now threatening the United States.[13]

In this increasingly unpredictable context the report did not argue in detail for the need for an ABM system, which is quite irrelevant and technically unworkable, and which in any case has divided the military. By late October 2001 the Pentagon was ready to postpone further tests indefinitely, a virtual admission that it had wasted tens of billions of dollars on unattainable technology—but then it backtracked. Testing of the ABM system has continued, but the results remain inconclusive, and there is even less reason to waste more funds on it. An effort was made after September 11 to get the Russians to acquiesce to changes in the 1972 treaty in return for alleged mutual reductions in strategic nuclear missiles, and the Bush administration shifted its tune from its implied willingness to unilaterally abrogate the treaty to getting Russia's assent to any changes. "I think it's enormously important that Russia look west," Rumsfeld commented in mid-November.[14] So long as there was a war in Afghanistan, the Russians were far more useful to the United States as friends, which momentarily gave them substantially more leverage in dealing with it. But as the war wound down, so too did the Bush administration's eagerness to get Moscow's agreement on crucial questions of security. In mid-December 2001, the Russians having served their usefulness, the United States renounced the 1972 treaty. But to abolish it for an ABM system that does not work is the height of folly—all liabilities and no assets. Even the Pentagon remains deeply divided on the ABM's practicality. But the president was much more motivated by principle than by practicality when he returned instinctively to the profound unilateralism which he began with, and he increased—and Congress approved—spending on the ABM to $8.3 billion, $3.1 billion more than the 2001 military budget. Not only Russia but the United States' traditional allies are likely to deplore it, but the message is clear: America is the sole superpower and can define the rules which govern the world.

It was not obvious, though, why the Pentagon's essentially traditional equipment and budgetary ambitions would solve the highly indefinable terrorist threat. The world was infinitely simpler for it when it had the Soviet Union to keep it preoccupied. The Chinese signed up via the World Trade Organization to be a part of the global capitalist economic system and were highly unlikely to get into a war with the United States—one they were certain to lose even if they destroyed America.

But in fact the Pentagon's hastily rewritten review only compounded the nation's problems, and it avoided confronting the sheer variety and complexity of the challenges now confronting the United States, much less why they existed in the first place. The location of challenges, the number of them, and even the identities of the specific enemies were left open. All that was certain was that bin Laden and al-Qaeda had to be brought to heel in the very near future but also that terrorism was a far larger and more geographically diverse problem, one that might take an indeterminate number of years to expunge—the president thought many years might be necessary to contain and solve the problem. Indeed, as Rumsfeld put it, "in the decades ahead, we will face other threats that seem just as unimaginable to us today." The surprises and threats were virtually permanent, made all the more likely, as Europe's intelligence officials warned last November, because American efforts may be creating more terrorists than they eliminate. Internal security would "become a permanent part of the way we live," Vice President Cheney stated in October 2001.[15]

There were no technological quick fixes, only sales of equipment—which are essential to companies, congressmen, and their constituents. Technological fetishism is an American malady, but solutions are political, and often economic also, or they are unsuccessful.

The End of the Conservative Economic Program

Events, not rational calculations, have determined how successive administrations have managed all crucial aspects of their foreign policy and economic programs, and they have adapted to the unintended, generally negative consequences of their actions far more than they will ever admit. Since 1947, all attempts to impose rational priorities on its policies and actions have floundered because of the United States' belief that it should become involved anywhere in the world it decides there is a problem, much less a crisis, in which its vaguely defined interests—such as economic or credibility—are at stake.

The September 11 trauma seemingly saved the Bush administration's attempt to reform the Pentagon and its budget from the same failure that was the fate of its predecessors. Now the civilians who run the Pentagon do not have to admit that they could not overcome the services' opposition to their grandiose organizational schemes. At the same time, it also covered its own profound incapacity to articulate a strategic plan that was relevant to the political and military realities of the twenty-first century. It could defer designating China as its likely future enemy, a step that was fraught with incalculable danger. The president and the Pentagon can now call a scruffy band of terrorists—desperate fanatics who exist in tiny numbers and in many places—their principal enemies for the indeterminate future. As problematic as the war in Afghanistan or against terrorism may seem in terms of lives and cost, much less the time and political complexities that the destabilization of South Asia and the Middle East may very well involve, it probably would have been at least as dangerous for the United States and the peace of the world had the Pentagon designated China as the major threat to America's welfare and existence. For not only is China far too powerful to be treated so contemptuously—but doing so would also have been a major error in judgment. The Chinese want primarily to do business, and in their own way and time China's leaders are discarding what little is left of their Leninist-Maoist heritage.

The Bush administration's economic program was also a victim of the September 11 events, and what was to be a conservative agenda has now been discarded in favor of what is best termed a variety of military Keynesianism. The bipartisan consensus in Congress not only eliminates many of the normal political processes but compounds the White House's problems because there is far less opposition—on both ends of the very narrow political spectrum—to the executive's doing as it wishes with the economy. The president is very powerful in all domains, not merely in the draconian restrictions on civil liberties he proposed but, above all, in the economy. There is a general mandate for the administration's loss of priorities, one that is inherent in what in the last analysis is consensus politics and the fact that the two parties share far more in common than divides them. The Enron scandal put Bush on the defensive, for the Democrats will seek to exploit it for political reasons, but the consensus that the two parties share remains far greater than their differences. Indeed, that these shifts have happened so easily makes it clear that Bush never had any sincere economic convictions to begin with, and that his conservative stance was merely designed to get himself nominated as the Republican presidential candidate.

The economy entered a recession in March 2001, the high-technology sector especially was in serious trouble, and it was very much a question whether Congress would support all the measures the president was nominally committed to. Tax rebates had no impact and commercial real estate was in the doldrums, while jobs were cut back and unemployment mounted to 5.8 percent in December 2001—substantially above the 4 percent for all of 2000. What the administration would do, given its initial fiscally conservative pledges, was very much in doubt. September 11 decided that.

The first problem after that tragic date was the huge losses in the stock market. The Federal Reserve cut interest rates, to slight effect, and provided $81 billion in liquidity to the financial markets in one day alone. Monetary policies might attain some goals, but they also carried huge risks, and unbalancing the economy was one of them. All sorts of rules to prevent manipulation and collusion were suspended. But the problems confronting the economy appeared far too complicated for easy solutions, and those who bought stock and expensive consumer goods were unprecedentedly pessimistic.

The airlines were quickly given a $15 billion package of cash and loan guarantees, and the insurers demanded aid too—in effect, making the taxpayers the insurers of last resort. They received important guarantees on future claims and damage, the exact form of which has yet to be determined, and Congress approved $55 billion in various emergency packages, including for the Pentagon, while it was negotiating as much as $100 billion in various economic stimuli with the White House. Now restaurants, filmmakers, theme parks, steelmakers, and even oil firms also wanted help, if only in the form of tax breaks. The administration attempted to call a halt to future bailouts, but a dangerous precedent has been set, and in economic difficulty many interests have political power. These were virtual subsidies to add to the long existing list.

But many of the president's budget proposals on domestic

affairs after September 11 soon became paralyzed, in part due to the Enron scandal and Democratic control of the Senate but mainly because his conservative biases and politically motivated and dubious budget projections and numbers put the administration on the defensive. In the meantime, the Pentagon's budget was increased 11.6 percent in 2002 and its share of the economy grew from 3.9 to 4.4 percent, reversing the post-1989 so-called peace dividend and giving it a windfall it had scarcely expected three months earlier. Even more money will go to pay for the war on terrorism, and at the beginning of 2002 the military services were told they should prepare for it to endure at least six more years. They, in turn, will ask for at least $20 billion more in fiscal 2003 than they otherwise expected, or $379 billion for the Pentagon.

In the spring of 2001 the president had promised a budget surplus of $236 billion for fiscal 2001, but it turned out to be $121 billion, or less than half of the preceding year's. And at the beginning of 2001 the Congressional Budget Office had projected a $5.6 trillion surplus over the next ten years, and the new president quickly enacted a $1.35 trillion tax cut over the decade based on these estimates; but now he faced far lower revenues and greater expenses. Indeed, congressional experts calculated that his tax cuts, from which upper-income earners were the main beneficiaries, in fiscal 2002 would be as much as twice the $60 billion the president had estimated. Instead of surpluses in 2002, his budget director in November 2001 predicted there would be $200 billion in deficits through fiscal 2004. At the beginning of 2002 some estimates of the promised ten-year surplus reduced it from $5.6 trillion to under $1 trillion, but if Social Security surpluses are excluded then the

10-year deficit will be $1.5 trillion, proving that such long-range projections are a highly speculative basis for tax cuts for the rich—which the president had already approved. Indeed, at the beginning of 2002 the administration asked Congress to quickly raise the debt ceiling limit from $5.95 trillion to $6.7 trillion. The government would have to borrow to cover deficits! The immense shortfall was a result of both the costs of September 11 and the recession that was well advanced before then.

Internationally, the picture was no better. Net capital flows to emerging markets fell $60 billion in 2001 and are expected to decline further. Money in loans and for debt relief would go to Pakistan—with $37 billion in foreign debts and nearly two-thirds of its budget revenues devoted to servicing it—and especially Turkey, America's Muslim allies. But Argentina was reluctantly deemed expendable by necessity, and it defaulted, with grave implications for Brazil and much of the rest of the hemisphere. There was a danger, respected Wall Street economists wrote, that the entire process of globalization of trade and growth could be halted, even reversed. That prospect existed before September 11, but it was made much more likely that the channels of trade would be clogged in unprecedented ways and that defense spending—and taxes—would also rise.

September 11 also marked the death of the conservative fiscal orthodoxy, with its advocacy of balanced budgets and elimination of subsidies. All the pillars of the conservative faith were crumbling, and overwhelming bipartisan approval of bailouts, public spending in the name of defense or fiscal stimulus, and projected deficits confirmed (if confirmation was needed) that conservatives were no more true to their articles of ideological faith than were liberals. Some congressional conservatives immediately accused Bush of compromising with the Democrats, and the president sought to assuage them with promises that he would cut his stimulus package to $75 billion—or $130 billion if one counts the direct costs attributed to September 11. But even most of these conservatives want favors for their powerful constituents, and some of their proposals for tax cuts go well beyond what even the president has advocated.

The truth was that despite the conservative pretensions of this administration virtually everyone in Washington had become a Keynesian, at least in the sense of favoring deficits. This in no way altered their deeply rooted belief that the United States is a model to the world, not the least bit inconsistent or hypocritical, and that free markets are the only efficient way to organize economies—a doctrine that academic economics has transformed into an absolute truth and that the IMF has attempted to implement in many dozens of nations. The United States is special. Rumsfeld typically stated this credo: "If one looked down from Mars on earth you would find that only a handful of countries are really capable of providing for their people, and where people provide for themselves . . . where the political and economic structures are such that the maximum benefit for the people is achieved." [16]

Getting ideology and practice to conform to each other is the historic contradiction of the American economy, beginning with the increasingly elaborate regulatory structure that was initiated at the end of the nineteenth century and continues today. These range from antidumping duties on imports and immense subsidies to upper-income groups (the top tenth of the farm recipients received two-thirds of the $72 billion in agricultural subsidies, 1996–2000) to tax advantages to upper-income earners, to name but a few of the departures from enshrined economic theory.

But public opinion—to repeat a crucial point—was with the president. His approval rating increased from a tepid 55 percent before September 11 to about 90 percent over the subsequent months. And while his father had the same experience after the Gulf War in 1991—and was defeated for reelection—for the time being Bush could let his conservatives brood over what was to them a betrayal of the true faith.

The president's ad hoc and essentially opportunistic economic measures showed clearly how events rather than rational priorities or ideology play the decisive role in guiding America's leaders in all domains, whether domestic policy or the military program and foreign policy. The present economic policies are very likely to produce further deficits and confusion in the economy. There was no consistency in President Bush's actions or ideas, but for the time being he was highly successful politically—and for a consummately ambitious politician, that is what counts most.

The Unilateral Presidency Reconsidered

Bush began his presidency with a policy of belligerent unilateralism, even worse than the Clinton administration's already provocative decisions, both ignoring and infuriating America's traditional allies. His most important step, by far, was the proposed ABM system, which has scant chance of protecting the United States against missiles but which axiomatically required the United States to repudiate its 1972 treaty on nuclear weapons with the USSR as well as the subsequent arms control treaties dependent on it. It did so at the end of 2001. That there would then be no restraints on testing by other nations and nuclear proliferation was less important than the administration's intention to resume American testing. The president's father in early 1993 had denounced the ban, which Congress had imposed upon him, and now his son was ready to end these restrictions. Since such a step makes the United States appear even more belligerent and unilateralist, it has also proposed alleged arms control measures which are wholly illusory and which Russia attacked as soon as they were made public at the beginning of 2002. The United States has about 6,000 deployed nuclear warheads and many thousands more which can be quickly readied. It now suggested it might reduce its operational warheads to about 3,800 in fiscal 2007 and to between 1,700 and 2,200 five years later, even though its intelligence informed it at the same time that the Russians would reduce their warheads to under 2,000 by 2015 with or without an arms agreement. But it would merely put these weapons on the shelf, not destroy them. It also made it clear that it was not bound to any numbers and felt free to shift its position at any time. More to the point, the United States would immediately annul the treaty banning nuclear testing—the real aim of its charade—and it would develop many more small nuclear weapons for first use against nonnuclear states, ranging from Iraq to Syria and Libya, under unpredictable conditions that would greatly increase the likelihood of America employing them.

Meanwhile, the president repudiated the Kyoto Protocol on global warming and the Biological Weapons Convention. The United States also opposed restrictions on offshore banking as well as further restrictions on testing nuclear weapons and land mines, or on manufacturing fissile materials—the list goes on and on. After September 11, however, the entire administration talked of new "floating" coalitions, "revolving coalitions that will evolve and change over time depending on the activity and the circumstances of the country. The mission needs to define the coalition." [17] What this meant, in great part, was an end to the NATO-based coalition, which in the Kosovo war had required inhibiting, time-consuming consultations and some measure of veto power by its members, especially the larger ones. This abandonment of NATO as a military organization was made explicit during 2002, when the United States proposed a simultaneous enlargement of its membership to include the Baltic states and to allow Russia to have a voice, though no veto regarding crucial matters. In effect, the Bush administration is prepared to reduce NATO to what will become a relatively innocuous political forum. A coalition must now accept Washington's objectives and work solely on its terms. It is, in effect, American unilateralism carried to its logical conclusion.

While I detail some of these problems in chapter 3, suffice it to say here that Washington and the Pentagon were still seething with frustration over how NATO, the organization the United States had created, fought its first real war by stymieing America's freedom to use its firepower any way it saw fit. And these frustrations only increased after September 11, because there is virtually no way the United States can engage in wars in any part of the world it chooses without depending on countries to allow it to do things and even help it. It still has to make compromises, and while Pakistan and Uzbekistan were two of the most crucial nations, they were hardly the only ones that imposed constraints on U.S. actions. Indeed, the United States needed effective Russian cooperation to fight the war in Afghanistan and against terrorism, and the idea of a unilateral renunciation of their 1972 treaty carried risks that had not existed earlier—at least not until it mastered the persistent, formidable technological limits of the antimissile system. Nations have interests, which often conflict, and this fact will never change. Moreover, as the September 11 events showed, America's definitions of its immediate interests will change dramatically and its need for allies along with it. But the fighting was not even over before the United States reneged on many of the solemn pledges it had made to its new allies. Still, there is simply no way the United States can intervene anywhere in the world without confronting traditional power and geopolitics. It is the price it must pay for its global ambitions. The only way to avoid paying it is for the United States to tailor its ambitions and accept the constraints that reality imposes on every nation, the United States included.

The United States utterly failed to anticipate its crisis after September 11, as indeed—to quote again Undersecretary Wolfowitz from June 2001—"the whole last century is littered with failures of prediction." It has not embarked on a new policy. Instead, it is trying to put other labels on its actions while relying on the remnants of its traditional approaches and ideas, of which the massive reliance on technology and firepower is the single most important. The Bush administration does not have a coherent foreign policy strategy. It is confused and has lost its bearings, and while its crusade against terrorism is politically very popular for the moment, even ignoring entirely the fickleness of voters, the real question is whether its new departure solves any meaningful foreign policy problems. Can the United States continue to take it upon itself to intervene everywhere in the hope of shaping the world to conform both to its vague ideals and, much more tangibly, to its interests? Even worse, do such interventions create far more problems for it than existed before?

The Islamic world is being increasingly polarized—as bin Laden intended. The inevitable legacies of a half century of U.S. policies and adventures in the Middle East have returned both to haunt the United States and to plunge it into a crisis. It is now unable to punish its adversaries without paying an increasingly mounting price at home. The events of September 11 and their aftermath prove this.

6

ANOTHER CENTURY OF WAR?

A foreign policy that is both immoral and unsuccessful is not simply stupid, it is increasingly dangerous to those who practice or favor it. That is the predicament that the United States now confronts.

Communism no longer exists, American military power has never been greater, but the United States has never been so insecure and its people more vulnerable. After fifty years of interventions in the affairs of dozens of nations on every continent (interventions that varied from training police and armies to supplying them with lethal equipment and advisers to teach them how to use it), and after two major wars involving its own manpower, America's sustained, intense, and costly efforts have only culminated in greater risks to itself. There is more instability and violence in the world than ever, and now they have finally reached America's own shores—and its political leaders have declared wars will continue. By any criterion, above all the security of its own citizens, the United States' international policies, whether military or political, have produced consummate failures. It is neither realistic nor ethical. Its foreign policy is a shambles of confusions and contradictions, pious, superficial morality combined with cynical adventurism, all of which has undermined, not strengthened, the safety of the American people and left a world more dangerous than ever.

It is not accurate, nor is it consolation, to argue as many do that without an activist foreign and military policy the present world situation could have been worse or that communism would have triumphed in many more places. Many of the CIA's analysts always perceived the Soviet Union's actions as essentially defensive, and that it was ready to grasp opportunities that posed no obvious dangers to it but was unwilling to take great risks. As Marxists they believed that history was predestined to favor them and that adventurism was unnecessary—"infantile," to use Lenin's description. But communism was a reflection rather than the cause of the severe disorder in international affairs that produced two incredibly destructive world wars. It was a result of deeper and older problems, and those who led the USSR gradually ceased to have the conviction essential to perpetuate the original Leninist beliefs and systemic legacies. As a ruling system, it has disappeared in Europe and virtually disintegrated in Asia, peacefully and by its own leaders' volition—and not by force of American arms.

The fear of communism which justified vast military expenses and mobilized NATO and America's allies is now gone, but the qualitative importance of this fundamental transformation has not led to any equivalent or appropriate changes in Washington's perceptions, much less spending. It can no longer define its enemies clearly, where they live or how they will behave, and it is unwilling to confront the analytic problems that the immense changes in world affairs since 1989 have created. The United States' most symbolic sites—Wall Street and the

Pentagon—have been devastatingly attacked, and it is now plain, as the government itself has predicted for several years, that the country itself is highly vulnerable. Bin Laden's network replaced "rogue states" for a time, but essentially American strategy continues to flounder: it prepared for nuclear and mechanized war in Europe but fought only in Asia, where it was stalemated and lost two major conflicts. It encouraged and funded wars by Iraq against Iran and against the Soviets in Afghanistan only to have to fight the very people it once believed were merely its proxies. It has confronted innumerable surprises in Latin America and Africa—to mention but a few of its policy failures—and it has precious little control in both those continents. The United States' ambitions in the century that is just beginning far exceed its military, political, and moral resources for attaining them, and if it does not acknowledge the limits of its power—which it should have done much earlier—it will continue to embark on quixotic adventures in every corner of the world . . . and experience more terrorism on its own shores.

The United States has more military equipment than ever, and since 1950 Pentagon spending has become one of the traditional and indispensable foundations of American prosperity. There is no indication that it will decline. But there are no technological quick fixes to political problems. Solutions are political. They require another mentality and much more wisdom, including a readiness to compromise and, above all, to stay out of the affairs of nations. Otherwise, they will not succeed. Worse yet, its reliance on weapons and force has exacerbated or created far more problems for the United States than it has solved. After September 11 there can be no doubt that arms have not brought security to America. It is not only in the world's interest that America adapt to the realities of the twenty-first century. What is new is that it is now, more than ever, in the interest of the American people themselves. It is imperative that the United States acknowledge the limits of its power—limits that are inherent in its own military illusions and in the very nature of a world that is far too big and complex for any country to even dream of managing.

Mankind cannot endure another century of war, because future wars will be far more destructive, to civilians as well as soldiers.

The Dangers of Mindless Action

Nations have differing interests and ways of perceiving them. The United States was belligerently unilateralist in the period before September 11 and changed briefly only to meet the grave emergency those events imposed upon it. It created "coalitions" which are ephemeral and transient marriages of convenience, essentially discarded NATO as the pillar of its European policy, and managed only to show that the United States is a fickle, unreliable partner. It is obviously quixotic if not dangerous to talk of coalitions when nations are unstable and perhaps even their rulers are in flux. It has already probably destabilized Pakistan and Saudi Arabia in the brief process of making war in Afghanistan, and in the years to come it will confront the consequences of having done so in these far more important countries.

The world is more violent, war-racked, and insecure than ever. Many American officials now nostalgically admit that the international system was far more predictable and safer when the USSR existed, precisely because it acted prudently. This nostalgia is largely misplaced, since many of the greatest problems that the world confronted after 1945 were quite independent of communism and persist even today; but it is also true that Moscow discouraged potentially dangerous confrontations to the extent that it could do so. The CIA told the government to expect the Soviets to behave cautiously, but its estimates were often ignored or disputed by military services—especially the air force—that wanted to justify more spending.

Indeed, the CIA and other official agencies gave successive presidents ample and accurate warnings of the risks they faced in Vietnam and elsewhere, but many of the warnings were ignored. Whatever rationality is built into the foreign affairs apparatus has had little impact in guiding policy makers since 1950. There was far less clarity among those who guided American foreign policy than there could have been, and those in charge were oblivious of either the consequences or even the goals of their actions. For them, action itself was the name of the game. And the world has paid for it. This essentially paranoid mentality failed to anticipate the collapse of the USSR, and it is still operational, for high budgets cannot be justified without dismal political prognostications, fear, and mysteries. Such thinking is unable to go beyond simplistic explanations, or to comprehend causes, or to understand the historical processes and social dynamics of countless nations. Now there is a paranoid view of Islam; the focus is off China temporarily, but it is the same vision.

There is far less understanding at the top than successive leaders have claimed, and domestic politics and short-term factors play a much greater role than they will ever admit. The world and now the American people cannot afford U.S. foreign policy's opportunistic and ad hoc character, its wavering between the immoral and the amoral in practice but that official speechwriters portray as rational and principled. In reality, it has neither coherence nor useful principles but often responds to one failure and crisis after another—and these are usually of its own making. Even given its unrealistic ambitions, it has lost control of its priorities, which all nations must have. We can never forget that the two men whom the United States has most demonized over the past two decades, Saddam Hussein and Osama bin Laden, both collaborated for years with it; Washington believed their causes were identical and put vast sums at their disposal. There is no greater proof of confusion and ineptness on America's part, and rather than leading the world in a better direction, it has usually inflicted incalculable harm wherever it has intervened. Its leaders have been addicted to intervening for its own sake, to save the nation's "credibility," to prevent an alleged vacuum of power, or to fulfill its self-appointed role as the enforcer of regional or global order (which it usually equates with the freedom of American businessmen to make money). The United States has refused to accept a much more modest and far less ambitious definition of its national interests, one that is also realistic.

All of its policies in the Middle East have been contradictory and counterproductive. The United States' support for Israel is the most important but scarcely the only cause of the September 11 trauma and the potentially fundamental political destabilization, ranging from the Persian Gulf to South Asia, that its intervention in Afghanistan has triggered. But it has repeatedly seen its most ambitious diplomatic and military efforts produce disasters instead. Its strategy of "triangulating" China and the Soviet Union, essentially to achieve a victory in Vietnam, backfired and accelerated its calamitous loss there. And there was Guatemala in 1953, Chile in 1973, Angola in 1975, and countless other places where its habitual penchant for activism and intervention produced acute disorders and thousands of deaths, and only perpetuated and usually aggravated many nations' difficulties.

There are many serious problems in the world that must be solved if there is to be much greater stability and peace: poverty, illiteracy, human rights, and the like. It was a convenient simplification for the Bush administration to blame al-Qaeda and "terrorism" for the world's insecurities and to pretend that resolving this challenge would lay to rest many, if not all, the others, everywhere. It will not. Moreover, America's military power is irrelevant for meeting virtually all of these issues, much less terrorism, and it was sheer opportunism for Washington to convey the impression that this was the major issue the United States now confronts. It is not. There are still countless unresolved problems in Latin America, Africa, and Asia that the United States cannot address, because it is wedded to approaches and institutions that have failed until now and will continue to do so in the future. There is no substitute for political and economic strategies that solve these real challenges rather than worry about what American businessmen and bankers think is in their interest. But since 1946 no administration has thought and acted this way. Instead, they have relied on military power to intervene countless times in various places to preserve status quos that perpetuate those economic and social conditions that lead to violence and terrorism.

Whatever its original intention, America's commitment of time and effort is essentially open-ended wherever it intervenes. It may last a short time, and often does, but complications can cause it to spend far more resources and time than it originally anticipated, causing it in the name of its "credibility" or some other doctrine that the government's publicists concoct, to get into situations that are disastrous and which in the end produce defeats for which the United States is much worse off. Vietnam is the leading example of this. Should it confront the forty or more nations that now have terrorist networks, then it will in one manner or another intervene everywhere, from Africa to the Middle East and Southeast Asia, and such commitments will be open-ended and unpredictable in terms of the time and effort each requires.

This lack of control causes America's leaders to lack coherence and lose priorities, because when wars begin their full consequences can never be predicted. This was true long before the United States became the preeminent global power, and it is still the case. Events over the past year have confirmed that destabilization and friends becoming enemies—and vice versa—are the rule in warfare and grand geopolitics, and to be expected. America's interventions since 1947 have usually not succeeded by the criteria it originally defined, and its security at the beginning of the twenty-first century is much more imperiled than it was fifty years ago.

The United States has more determined and probably more numerous enemies today than ever, and many of those who hate it are ready and able to inflict death and destruction on its shores. Its interventions often triumphed in the purely military sense, which is all the Pentagon worries about; but they have been political failures in too many cases and have led to yet more interventions. Its virtually instinctive activist mentality has led it to leap into situations where it often had no interests, much less durable solutions, and where it has repeatedly created disasters and enduring enmities. America has power without wisdom, and cannot recognize the limits of arms despite its repeated experiences. The result has been folly, and hatred, which is a recipe for disasters. September 11 confirmed that. The war has come home.

The United States can no longer afford procrastination or to commit more errors, much less continue the ad hoc, immoral, confused opportunism that has guided Washington for a half century. It cannot throw money at the Pentagon as if more weapons solve rather than aggravate political problems. It has been adrift for decades, and has refused to admit that its interventions have failed to resolve—and have usually exacerbated—most, if not all, of the challenges that Washington for almost fifty years has used to justify sending men, machines, and money to every corner of the world. Its readiness to pursue activist military and foreign policies has, if anything, intensified most of the world's problems by encouraging—and giving the essential material means—to tyrants and officers who satisfy America's definitions of its own interests. These proxies resist essential social and economic changes, and their adventurism should be discouraged. We see today in the Persian Gulf and Afghanistan how such ambitions have failed, probably catastrophically, but on a smaller scale there are countless other places where U.S. intervention has left festering problems that are returning to haunt and endanger it.

But by purely nonideological, rational criteria U.S. foreign policies have failed even if they have made the world more prosperous for its own businessmen and investors and their local cronies. The American people are now paying the price in lives lost and permanent insecurity—and they will have to accept the turbulent existence that the president after September 11 promised.

At the present juncture of history, wars are at least as likely as at any time over the past century. The end of Soviet hegemony in Eastern Europe and of Moscow's restraining influence elsewhere is only one factor, albeit of great importance. The proliferation of nuclear technology and other means of mass destruction has made large parts of the world much more dangerous, while highly destructive local wars with conventional weapons in Africa, the Balkans, the Middle East, and elsewhere have only multiplied since the 1960s. Europe, especially Germany, and Japan are far stronger and more independent than at any time since 1945, and China's burgeoning economy has given it a vastly more important role in Asia.

The world is more complex and dangerous than it was during the cold war. The decentralization of military and political power, and the obduracy of the United States' ambitions to guide the destinies of a virtually unlimited number of nations, are a highly inflammable mixture. The United States has become what establishment pillar Samuel P. Huntington aptly calls the only "rogue superpower," full of dual standards and hypocrisy in its pretensions to be "the indispensable nation," as he quotes Madeleine K. Albright, committed to advancing "universal values"—as another State Department official he cites put it.[1] America has repeatedly sought to impose those values and policies that conform to its definitions and interests on nations and international organizations. This has led it, on the one hand, to lofty proclamations and, on the other, to protecting American corporate interests, buttressing tyrants, selling or giving arms to nations that have rebellious populations or grievances against neighboring states, and unilaterally bullying its allies as well as weaker enemies. September 11 proves it is no longer immune to the destructive consequences of these designs. It must change fundamentally or pay a frightful, ever mounting price. That price is a function both of its foreign policies and of the spread and intensity of weapons of mass destruction. There are a sufficient number of people, quite independent of states, who are ready to use the latter.

All factors considered—the breakup of Yugoslavia, events in Africa and the Middle East, to name but a few—wars, both civil or between states, remain the principal (but scarcely the only) challenge facing much of humanity in the twenty-first century. The numerous ecological disasters affecting all dimensions of the environment are equally insidious because of their gradual but relentless development and the unwillingness of the crucial nations—above all, the United States—to adopt measures essential for reversing the damage. In many vital regards, the challenges facing humanity have never been so complex and threatening, and there is not the slightest reason for complacency or optimism as a result of the end of the cold war.

It is a precondition of stemming, much less reversing, the accumulated deterioration of world affairs that the United States end its self-appointed global mission of regulating all problems, wherever, whenever, or however it wishes to do so. There are countless ethical and other reasons to cease meddling everywhere. It has no more right or capacity to do so than any state over the past century. But September 11 confirmed, if any confirmation was needed, that the United States has abysmally failed to bring peace and security to the world. Instead, it has managed to become increasingly hated, placing itself in profound and mortal danger. But an additional reason for ending its role as a rogue superpower and its promiscuous, cynical interventionism is pragmatic: it has been spectacularly unsuccessful even on its own terms, it is squandering vast economic resources, and it now places the physical security of Americans on their own soil in danger. Paramount are the obligations that politicians have to their own citizens, and to cease the damage the United States causes abroad is also to fulfill their responsibilities to their own people. Neither the American population nor its political leaders are likely to agree to such far-reaching changes in foreign policy, and there is not the slightest sign at this point that voters will call their politicians to account; but more events of the order of the September 11 calamity or the anthrax scare may produce a learning process—and eventual changes.

Communism and fascism were products of the grave errors in the international order and affairs of states that the First World War created, and the Soviet system disintegrated after sixty years because it was the aberrant consequence of a very destructive war. But radicalized, suicidal Islamists are, to a great extent, the outcome of a half century of America's interference in the Middle East and the Muslim world: its repeated grave errors, however different the contexts or times, have produced their own abnormal, negative reactions. It is under these conditions and with these threats that our century has begun. There are yet other crises incubating. Above all, the destructive potential of weaponry has increased exponentially, and many more people and nations have access to it, so that what would once have been considered small foreign policy problems now have potentially far greater consequences. It all augurs very badly.

There will be serious problems throughout much of the world even if the United States abstains from interference and tailors its actions to fit this troubled reality. Internecine civil conflicts will continue, as well as wars between states armed with a growing variety of much more destructive weapons supplied by outside powers, of which the United States remains, by far, the leader. Many of these conflicts have independent roots, but the arguments for America's staying out of them should be dictated by both principles and experiences.

The way America's leaders are running the nation's foreign policy is not creating peace or security at home or stability abroad. The reverse is the case: its interventions have been counterproductive. Everyone—Americans and those people who are the objects of their efforts—would be far better off if the United States did nothing, closed its bases overseas and withdrew its fleets everywhere, and allowed the rest of the world to find its own way without American weapons and troops. Communism is dead, and Europe and Japan are powerful and can take care of their own affairs as they think best. There is every reason for the United States to adapt to these facts; to continue as it has over the past half century is to admit it has the vainglorious and irrational ambition to run the world.

It cannot. It has failed in the past and it will fail in this century, and attempting to do so will inflict wars and turmoil on many nations as well as on its own people.

SOURCES AND NOTES

The following is a selection of general works and sources that are especially useful. I have used the full text of statements and newspapers extensively, and some are cited below, but I have also relied on the *Los Angeles Times,* which I consider the best American daily, and foreign press translations in the weekly *Courrier International.*

I have written four books that are especially relevant to this work. For a history of American interventions, see my *Confronting the Third World: United States Foreign Policy, 1945–1980* (New York, 1988); for modern wars and their meaning, see my *Century of War: Politics, Conflicts, and Society Since 1914* (New York, 1994); for the Vietnam War, see my *Anatomy of a War: Vietnam, the United States, and the Modern Historical Experience* (New York, 1994); general background, coauthored with Joyce Kolko, is in *The Limits of Power: The World and United States Foreign Policy, 1945–1954* (New York, 1972).

For the role of intelligence, very insightful are Richard J. Aldrich, *The Hidden Hand: Britain, America and Cold War Secret Intelligence* (London, 2001); Robert M. Gates, *From the Shadows: The Ultimate Insider's Story of Five Presidents and How They Won the Cold War* (New York, 1996); and especially the former head of the CIA's Soviet estimates, Willard C. Matthias, *America's Strategic Blunders: Intelligence Analysis and National Security Policy, 1936–1991* (University Park, Pa., 2001); Harold P. Ford, *CIA and the Vietnam Policymakers: Three Episodes, 1962–1968* (CIA Center for the Study of Intelligence, 1998).

For Afghanistan, in addition to the books cited, see also O. S. Westad, "Concerning the Situation in 'A': New Russian Evidence on Soviet Intervention in Afghanistan," *Cold War International History Project Bulletin,* nos. 8–9 (winter 1996–97), pp. 128–84; the following collections of the National Security Archive: "Volume I: Terrorism and U.S. Policy," September 21, 2001; "Afghanistan: The Making of U.S. Policy, 1973–1990," October 5, 2001; "Volume II: Afghanistan: Lessons from the Last War," Oct. 9, 2001, especially the essay by Steve Galster; "Volume IV: The Once and Future King?," October 26, 2001, as well as other document collections the National Security Archive has released.

For the Middle East, in addition to the books cited above, see Kamran Asdar Ali, "Pakistan's Dilemma," September 19, 2001, Middle East Research and Information Project, and MERIP's work in general and especially the MERIP PINs, available at http://merip.org/; Christopher Deliso, "Bin Laden, Iran, and the KLA: How Islamic Terrorism Took Root in Albania," September 19, 2001, available at www.antiwar.com; the series on Saudi Arabia by Robert G. Kaiser and David B. Ottaway in the *Washington Post,* February 10–12, 2002; Yezid Sayigh, *Armed Struggle and the Search for State: The Palestinian National Movement, 1949–1993* (Oxford, 1997); and especially Gilles Kepel, *Jihad: Expansion et déclin de l'islamisme* (Paris, 2000).

Other useful books are Barry M. Blechman and Stephen S. Kaplan, *Force Without War: U.S. Armed Forces as a Political Instrument* (Washington, 1978); Dilip Hiro, *The Longest War: The Iran-Iraq Military Conflict* (New York, 1991); and especially Chalmers Johnson, *Blowback: The Costs and Consequences of American Empire* (New York, 2000).

The following code abbreviations are used in the notes:

DoD U.S. Department of Defense. The Pentagon calls them "News Briefings," "Interviews," "News Transcript," and such. The personality and date are all that is essential; there are other DoD documents for which I give compete citations. All official sources are found on the Web site: www.defenselink.mil

DS U.S. Department of State. All official sources are found on the Web site: www.state.gov

FT *Financial Times*

IHT *International Herald Tribune*

NYT *The New York Times*

WH If alone, it indicates the president's speech. Press briefings are indicated as "WH press briefing." All official sources are found on the Web site: www.whitehouse.gov/

WP *The Washington Post*

CHAPTER 1
THE WAR COMES HOME

1. Bush speech to Congress, WH, September 20, 2001; *WP,* October 21, 2001; WH press briefing, September 18, 2001.
2. *IHT,* October 18, 2001; *WP,* September 20, 2001; Rumsfeld, DoD, November 14, 2001; *The Guardian* (London), November 10, 2001; WH, November 6, 2001.
3. WH, November 21, 2001.
4. Rumsfeld, DoD, October 24, 2001.
5. *WP,* November 7, 2001, November 28, 2001.
6. *WP,* September 27, 2001.
7. U.S. Army, "Posture Statement," May 1999, p. vii; CIA, "Global Trends 2015," December 2000, p. 39; Cohen, DoD, July 5, 2000.

8. WH, November 6, 2001.
9. IHT, November 22, 2001.
10. Robert S. Gelbard, press conference, DS, February 23, 1998.

CHAPTER 2
THE MIDDLE EAST:
THE LEGACIES OF FAILURE

1. Gabriel Kolko and Joyce Kolko, *The Limits of Power: The World and United States Foreign Policy, 1945–1954* (New York, 1972), p. 341 and passim. Very useful for all aspects of Anglo-American tensions is Richard J. Aldrich, *The Hidden Hand: Britain, America and Cold War Secret Intelligence* (London, 2001).
2. Gabriel Kolko, *Confronting the Third World: United States Foreign Policy, 1945–1980* (New York, 1988), pp. 70, 72.
3. Ibid., p. 73.
4. Ibid., p. 81.
5. Ibid., pp. 85–88.
6. For every aspect of this conflict, see Dilip Hiro, *The Longest War: The Iran-Iraq Conflict* (New York, 1991); and his *Neighbors, Not Friends: Iraq and Iran After the Gulf Wars* (London, 2001), pp. 27–34.
7. Quoted in my *Century of War* (New York, 1994), p. 448.
8. All data are from U.S. Energy Information Administration, "Persian Gulf Oil and Gas Exports Fact Sheet," February 2001, passim.

CHAPTER 3
THE TRAP: AFGHANISTAN AND
THE UNITED STATES

1. Robert A. Flaten to Mr. Laingen, May 31, 1972, in "Volume IV: The Once and Future King?" National Security Archive, October 26, 2001.

2. Robert M. Gates, *From the Shadows: The Ultimate Insider's Story of Five Presidents and How They Won the Cold War* (New York, 1996), pp. 144–45; Brzezinski interview reprinted in *Counterpunch,* October 8, 2001.

3. Gates, *From the Shadows,* p. 145.

4. See ibid., p. 132; O. S. Westad, "Concerning the Situation in 'A': New Russian Evidence on Soviet Intervention in Afghanistan," *Cold War International History Project Bulletin,* nos. 8–9 (winter 1996–97), pp. 129–30 and passim.

5. *FT,* November 28–30, 2001, has a special series on al-Qaeda that is extremely informative. See also Gates, *From the Shadows,* pp. 319–21; *NYT,* December 21, 2001; and especially Gilles Kepel, *Jihad: Expansion et déclin de l'islamisme* (Paris, 2000), pp. 334 ff.

6. Gates, *From the Shadows,* p. 433.

7. WH, June 25, 1999.

8. DoD, "Report to Congress, Kosovo/Operation Allied Force After-Action Report," January 31, 2000, p. 5.

9. Cohen, DoD, December 5, 2000.

10. *IHT,* March 24–25, 2001; *NYT,* July 14, 2001.

11. *NYT,* October 13, 2001.

12. *FT,* October 12, 2001.

13. Rumsfeld, DoD, November 20, 2001.

14. *IHT,* November 22, 2001, November 26, 2001.

15. Rumsfeld, DoD, November 7, 2001; Powell, DS, October 10, 2001.

16. Rumsfeld, DoD, November 14, 2001.

17. *Boston Globe,* October 22, 2001.

18. *FT,* November 5, 2001.

19. Rumsfeld, DoD, September 25, 2001, September 27, 2001.

20. *WP,* October 21, 2001; Rumsfeld, DoD, October 24, 2001.

CHAPTER 4
THE MAKING OF AMERICAN FOREIGN
POLICY: SUCCESSES, AND FAILURES

1. I take up these questions in my *Century of War: Politics, Conflicts, and Society Since 1914* (New York, 1994), and, with Joyce Kolko, *The Limits of Power: The World and United States Foreign Policy, 1945–1954* (New York, 1972).
2. See my *Confronting the Third World* (New York, 1988), pp. 51–52.
3. Barry M. Blechman and Stephen S. Kaplan, *Force Without War: U.S. Armed Forces as a Political Instrument* (Washington, 1978), pp. 33, 556.
4. I discuss the Vietnam War in extensive detail in my *Anatomy of a War: Vietnam, the United States, and the Modern Historical Experience* (New York, 1994).
5. There is a large substantiating literature. See, for example, Gabriel Kolko, "Ravaging the Poor: The International Monetary Fund Indicted by Its Own Data," *Multinational Monitor*, June 1998, pp. 20–23; James C. Knowles et al., "Social Consequences of the Financial Crisis in Asia: The Deeper Crisis," *Manila Social Forum* (Asian Development Bank, November 9–12, 1999, conference); Martin Ravallion, "Growth, Inequality and Poverty: Looking Beyond Averages," World Bank Working Paper 2558, February 26, 2001, p. 21.

CHAPTER 5
STRATEGIC CONFUSIONS

1. Wolfowitz, DoD, August 16, 2001, June 14, 2001.
2. DoD, "1996 Annual Defense Report," chapter 1: "The Defense Strategy and the National Security Strategy," pp. 1, 4–5, 12–13, May 19, 1997.

3. Lt. Gen. Patrick M. Hughes, statement to Senate Select Committee on Intelligence, January 28, 1998, p. 3.

4. DoD, *Quadrennial Defense Review Report,* September 30, 2001, pp. 1–2.

5. David C. Gompert and Jeffrey A. Isaacson, "Planning a Ballistic Missile Defense System of Systems," *Rand Issue Paper,* 1999, p. xx.

6. Cohen, DoD, July 5, 2000.

7. DoD, "The United States Security Strategy for the East Asia–Pacific Region," November 23, 1998, pp. 4, 11.

8. *IHT,* January 12, 2001.

9. Rumsfeld, DoD, July 24, 2001, July 30, 2001; Wolfowitz in *Washington Times,* August 29, 2001.

10. *WP,* July 14, 2001; Wolfowitz, DoD, August 16, 2001.

11. Wolfowitz, DoD, September 14, 2001; DoD, *Quadrennial Defense Review Report,* September 30, 2001, p. 4.

12. Rumsfeld, DoD, October 12, 2001.

13. Rumsfeld, DoD, September 30, 2001; DoD, *Quadrennial Defense Review Report,* p. iv and passim.

14. DoD, November 14, 2001.

15. *IHT,* November 2, 2001; *WP,* October 21, 2001.

16. Rumsfeld, DoD, October 12, 2001.

17. Rumsfeld, DoD, September 25, 2001; Rumsfeld in *NYT,* as released by the DoD, September 27, 2001.

CHAPTER 6
ANOTHER CENTURY OF WAR?

1. Samuel P. Huntington, "The Lonely Superpower," *Foreign Affairs* (March–April 1999), pp. 37–38.

INDEX